Surviving Blake

A memoir by **Perpetual** Survivor

Based on a true story

Acknowledgments

I owe a great deal of thanks to several people who helped me write this book. Ken Scott, who helped me piece my initial recollections together into something more readable. Tony Horne (http://www.secretsofaghostwriter.com) who gave me comments on things I needed to add more details about and provided advice on how to structure a book for best readability. Joan Elliott, who diligently cleaned up the wording to improve final readability and prompted me to provide additional insight into my internal thoughts and reactions to what was happening; even guessing about things Blake had done that I had not pieced together myself. Michael Sandlin gave me a last-minute rapid-paced proofread to ensure a smooth reading experience. Finally, thanks go to Tadeo Phillips who created a custom piece of art to my approximate specifications for the cover.

Due to the nature of the book, I also owe thanks to all those who helped me survive. There are quite a few who will go unmentioned, but my martial arts instructors provided the seeds of knowledge necessary to stay alive. My parents, close family and college friends who provided perpetual love and support, even if they had difficulty believing some of it. The gods, spirits, mystics or whatever else it was that saw me through it all and absolutely had to have a hand in helping me survive.

I also wanted to offer some apologies to those I've hurt along the way. Blake left me in a rather crazed state, and I haven't been the easiest to work with at times, especially when I initially became single (I was kind of crazed by all of this) and whenever my safety was endangered (I was just trying to stay alive and dealing with it all alone). I also know there were some ancient mistakes I made before Blake. I'm sorry to those I've hurt and will endeavor to be better in the future.

I feel I can't leave this section without casting shade on the horrid people who attacked me for made-up reasons without validating the motives behind what they did, especially those who just ruin lives for fun. The latter are criminals who hurt me and will continue to hurt other people in the future. I'm sorry I didn't follow up on events well enough to shut them down. Perhaps this book will help deliver some justice to protect others from them in the future.

I don't want to end this on a bad note though, so I'll instead end on intrigue. I'll therefore thank the lady who handed me wings and the forgiving understanding person who had them constructed.

Thanks to all my readers. Please feel free to reach out with constructive criticism or other comments to perpetualsurvivor82@gmail.com. And if you like it, **please leave a decent review**. As a first-time author, I rely on readers like you to attract others to my work.

Preface

This book details my relationship with my ex-husband, known here as Blake. I describe the terrifying life situations that he created for me and provide details about the circumstances surrounding his untimely death a few weeks before Christmas. I will briefly touch on the events after. I may eventually provide a follow-up book that encompasses more of my life outside of my relationship with Blake.

This is based on a true story. I have done my best to accurately recall events and explain them clearly from my perspective. I've avoided referencing specific years and changed some names and locations to preserve anonymity. I did try to provide a general reference to the passage of time.

I don't recall everything, but to the best of my knowledge, this is how I remember the parts of my story that I've decided to share.

1.Spider

This is a story that Blake told me. I have no way to verify the story; unless someone can find the people who picked him up.

Blake had parachuted into a spot in Afghanistan with a few other soldiers. He never mentioned their mission, but all his fellow troops had been killed in action; he didn't discuss how he was the only survivor. Blake had seven days to cross an enormous distance alone through the desert to get to his pickup point. Not a great position to be in within enemy territory. He didn't know the land very well and had to navigate using equipment while keeping an eye out for potential insurgents and wildlife he knew nothing about.

On the first night, Blake was eating his dinner under a small grove of trees, planning to hide near the brush to get some sleep. While enjoying his meal, an enormous spider came to join him. It stopped a reasonable distance from him and watched him eating. Blake didn't react in fear to the spider. It wasn't acting aggressively, but was staring at his food intently and seemed interested. Blake said that he decided he needed a friend, any friend. This one would do. He threw it some meat and watched it eat greedily. When it was done, it disappeared into the brush. At the very least, his actions might keep the spider from killing him in his sleep.

Blake noticed a similar-looking spider in his general vicinity throughout the next day. He eventually realized it was the same one; it was following him at a distance. That evening, Blake fed the spider more meat and his new companion again disappeared into a thicket overnight. He officially had a friend and was no longer alone. Eventually, Blake let it follow along more closely. He continued to feed it at every meal. Just one small chunk of meat, not enough that he would go hungry. The rations were disgusting anyway. The spider spent another quiet night and day with Blake.

On the fourth evening, Blake made camp and lay down to sleep. As he was resting there, three insurgents (or angry locals) snuck up on his camp and took him captive. They were deciding whether to kill or imprison him.

Suddenly, the spider jumped out of a tree and bit one man on the neck. The resulting panic created enough chaos that Blake successfully killed the remaining two while the one who had been bitten turned blue and asphyxiated.

Blake slept not far from the corpses that night, an experience that would disturb almost anyone. He started sharing a second chunk of meat with the spider from there on and after another few days, made it to the pickup point where a man in a helicopter greeted him. He first had to explain what happened to the rest of his unit. Then, he was hoping to keep his new friend.

"Hey, this spider here killed a man and saved my life; mind if I take him with us?"

"What, are you crazy? Those things are poisonous! No, you can't take that thing aboard."

He said he wondered what happened to that spider from time to time; its memory, and his appreciation for what it did never left him.

2. Bear

This chapter is about me and just as unbelievable. I was considering not including it due to the fact that I can't validate it, and it might have been a fantasy, but it fits too well with Blake's spider story to exclude and sets up a nice contrast of characters by introducing me prior to meeting Blake.

I had a job as a data analyst/consultant for public service agencies; we primarily worked with child welfare organizations, but there were a few public assistance agencies and specialty courts thrown into the mix. I lived in upstate New York (N.Y.), but they flew me all over the country for various contracts. On three separate trips, I had the opportunity to work in Alaska; the longest was for a month. This story most likely occurred on the first trip, after several days camping and kayaking in Glacier Bay.

Shortly before flying back home, I decided to go on a hike and picked a random trail to walk on; it was unfamiliar terrain to me, so it wasn't very important where I hiked. I just chose a trail that was drivable from my hotel. It was on the edge of a small town. The parking lot was empty except for my car, and the forest was entirely devoid of people other than myself. Being alone was a welcome reprieve to clear my head.

After about three miles of walking, I left the forest behind and found the base of a mountain. There were a lot of rocks and I tripped, injuring my foot. It wouldn't hold any weight, and there was no cellphone signal. The rocky section of the trail had no sticks to use as a support, so there was no way to create a splint or crutch. I had no choice but to drag myself back—for now, at least.

I was forcefully pulling myself along the thankfully flat, well-cleared trail for perhaps five minutes. I knew I would eventually get back to the main forest and that there would be some kind of crutch available to walk with. My backpack had one meat stick and a granola bar left to eat.

Suddenly, a colossal bear crossed the trail in front of me about fifteen feet away. Lying on my belly with my head up, I stopped as it looked over at me. The bear observed me for a moment as fear filled my heart. There was no time to think. How should I react to this? Running away was clearly not an option, and my black belt in Tang Soo Do would be of no use, even without an injury. I was helpless, all alone in the woods facing death by bear. Trying to scare it off might anger it and provoke an attack where one wouldn't have taken place otherwise. The bear seemed more curious than hungry or aggressive. My intuition was telling me I was safe. It certainly didn't act threatened. Deciding to play pathetic, I rolled on my side and pointed at my ankle while whimpering.

As it approached, I stayed still, feeling nervous but oddly confident that she wouldn't hurt me. I'm not sure why, other than to say that her body language was peaceful, relaxed, and curious. She seemed concerned about me as she came over and sniffed my ankle. I held out my hand and let her sniff it. She then walked behind me, grabbed my collar with her mouth, and started to drag me along the trail, in the direction of the small town. I decided she was most likely helping me get back to the parking lot. Either way, it was the right direction and maybe we would run into a person. We were at least making better headway together. An anxious trust developed within me.

After some time, our movement proved to be difficult for both of us. She was not able to keep a good grip, and we kept needing to stop. Yanking on my neck was not the best feeling either. We had gotten back to the forest and there were bulky roots on the trail that were difficult to negotiate and painful for her to pull me over. We passed a heavy, flat piece of wood next to the trail, so I pulled my collar out of the bear's mouth and waved to make it clear I wanted to stop. She turned with a slight look of confusion on her face.

I crawled over to the piece of wood and used it to create something more like a pallet while the bear watched. Fortunately, the process of becoming an Eagle Scout had taught me how to tie knots. Using long dried grass as rope, I set it up so she could drag me while lying on the flat piece of wood. My new friend immediately recognized my intention and grabbed the makeshift rope to pull me along. This went much more quickly as it glided over the roots easily. We were making better progress. Truthfully, it was possible to make a crutch at this point, but I was now amused at being dragged by a bear. A delicate trust and friendship had developed at this point.

We managed to get halfway back by nightfall. There was still no phone signal, nor had we encountered other people. We made camp right on the trail. I pulled out my remaining snacks and ate my granola bar. When I opened the meat bar, she looked over at me, so I offered her some. Her body tensed up, and she suddenly looked angry and offended.

She sniffed in my direction, and her thoughts seemingly went through my mind. They said, *Don't you think I'd eat you if I ate meat? That had better not be bear meat.* I became briefly worried that my offense would be my undoing. Would I die now, or would she just stomp off? She seemed to sigh and kind of shrugged it off as she disappeared into the woods, but it was hard to tell. Finishing the meat snack and feeling kind of guilty about it, I was mostly relieved she didn't attack me and wondered if she would return. Sleep was necessary either way, and maybe my foot would feel better in the morning. It would be a much easier drag back here, and I figured there was plenty of wood to use as a crutch at the very least. My stomach growled.

After some time, the bear came back and handed me a large handful of blueberries. It would have been rude not to take them, so I ate them feeling grateful, but obviously with some trepidation. They were delicious and helped stave off hunger for the night. There were no regrets as I slept next to my new friend for warmth and trusted this wonderful creature completely at this point. Her name would be Bertha, Bertha the bear.

In the morning, we resumed our trip back. The pallet fell apart at some point, and there wasn't enough surplus wood around for me to fix it or make another one. We were not far from the parking lot at this point though, and the trail was relatively smooth. So, we battled on, her pulling me by the collar of my coat.

At long last, we came to a clearing, and the parking lot was visible down a moderately sized hill. I felt so relieved seeing that it was only a half mile back to my car and human civilization. Almost there! We stopped briefly to appreciate the journey we had just taken together before Bertha resumed. About halfway there, a man in the lot saw us. He reacted with shock, jumping in place and backward slightly as he took in a scene he had likely never seen before: a man being dragged by a bear. Grabbing a shotgun from his truck in panic, he started running in our direction. He shot the gun in the air three times, terrifying both of us.

"No, please don't shoot her! She saved my life! Please!"

"Bears don't do that. She has some nefarious purpose in mind." He continued running toward us, shooting the gun in the air.

"No really! I slept next to her! She fed me! I think she's an ethical vegan!"

"That's crazy. Bears don't help people. I don't believe you."

I motioned for Bertha to run back to the woods, but she hesitated, fearing the man with me, perhaps—or maybe just needing a second to decide. I slapped her rump to encourage her to go and felt terror, both for her safety and my own because there was no telling how she would react to being hit. Fortunately, my friend ran away as the man continued to fire the gun in the air but in her general direction.

"No! Please! Please don't hurt her!"

"I'm just scaring it off."

Watching her run up the hill, knowing I would never see her again, there was regret at not collecting some form of video evidence and a profound sadness that I would probably never see her again. The man called an ambulance for me, and paramedics provided medical care. I don't recall the nature of the injury, but I have a vague recollection of using crutches for a short period of time back in N.Y. I probably would have survived without Bertha, but it sure was fun and mystical being dragged by a bear.

3. Meeting Blake

Half a decade later, I had a new job working as a consultant/programmer for a large international firm. I was permanently stationed with a New York State agency when I met Blake via Adam4Adam; a gay dating app. It was the morning before my birthday, near the end of summer. There was a facility to register a wink to guys that you liked the look of, and Blake had winked at me sometime overnight.

Blake's profile was basically empty. It mentioned that he was also 25 years old and 5'11" but a bit heavier than me at 165 lbs. It lacked a description, which is not uncommon because it's so difficult to describe yourself in a hundred characters or fewer. There was not very much in my profile either; a picture of my smiling face, poofy curls and stats: 25 years old, 5'11", 125 lbs. It probably mentioned I was a programmer.

We had an almost cursory conversation online, but my fridge was empty and I had woken up hungry knowing a grocery store trip was in order. It was a bit late in the morning, so I invited him to meet me for lunch at a restaurant that was an eight-minute walk from my apartment. Blake immediately said, "Great, I look forward to it!" I noticed that he was quite far away and was briefly suspicious because it was kind of an inconvenient drive for someone you had barely chatted with. But I was still waking up and didn't think much about it.

We said, "See you later." I jumped in the shower and started to get ready. Feeling positive about meeting someone for a meal instead of dining alone, I killed a little time and relaxed for a while on the couch. Just before one in the afternoon, I walked up the hill toward the restaurant while wondering what Blake might be like. These dating sites are quite shallow and cannot reveal the actual nature of the person behind the profile. Nobody is going to list their bad attributes, are they? Generally, one chats a bit longer. This had been such a brief conversation.

Would he be an interesting person? Would he just be another new friend, or perhaps more? The trouble with dating sites is that you could be meeting up with a real crazy person. My black belt made me feel confident about handling any form of assault, and he had no way of knowing where I lived. This made me feel relatively comfortable despite my small stature compared with Blake.

We met outside the restaurant, and I noticed that Blake was attractive. He also presented himself quite well, dressing a bit more formally than my casual attire, without being over the top. The hostess sat us at a table for two directly next to a middle-aged couple. The four of us were the only diners in the restaurant; in hindsight, we probably should have asked for a table further away from them.

I quickly noticed that Blake liked to speak loudly so others could hear, and neither the couple nor the restaurant staff would have guessed we were on a date when we walked in. The couple would soon find out. We were not far from the few local gay bars, but my general impression was that most people were not entirely comfortable around a gay couple. I typically prefer to remain quiet and unobtrusive; Blake's brazenness made me slightly uncomfortable. Knowing a straightlaced couple was listening may have slightly influenced the way I reacted to a few of his queries.

I most likely slouched slightly in my chair with terrible posture. I did not know this then, but I have a mild connective tissue disorder that makes it more difficult to sit up straight because the stuff that glues me together is slightly weaker than normal. It makes my body a bit harder to care for than most because it causes generalized delicacy. I was used to ignoring randomized pain as it had started during elementary school, and the advice I had received from doctors was never very helpful. I have since learned the importance of good posture and should have started sooner, but some lessons in life take time to learn.

Blake discussed his army background, boasting about being highly decorated, including having received a Purple Heart. Specifics were lacking, but I knew the Purple Heart was a military decoration awarded to those wounded or killed while serving in the U.S. military. A custom dating back to the American Revolutionary War. He explained that he had moved back home from Chicago to help his grandmother when she was ill but that she had passed recently, so he was deciding the next direction for his life.

We talked about ambitions and dreams. All Blake ever wanted to do was to be a musician and mentioned that he had a plan to attend a local music school. He played the organ at a church slightly north of Albany. I told him about playing the trombone in 5th and 6th grade. My music career ended abruptly after determining the mile journey to and from school with a heavy trombone case and textbooks was warping my young back. No matter my skill or enjoyment at playing: it just wasn't worth the back pain caused by the journey.

I talked about my career as a programmer and mentioned that I worked for New York State through a consulting firm. As well as my half-Jewish heritage, I also mentioned that I was not raised religiously and did not have any form of faith or practice outside my own loosely held belief structure.

Blake next inquired about open relationships and almost seemed to project the inquiry toward the heterosexual couple sitting next to us. This made me fairly uncomfortable because the standards are so different. Women have a general proclivity to find a single man to mate with and help her raise a child, whereas men tend to have an urge to spread the seed around. On top of that, the cultural biases associated with promiscuous women are so negative; they are heavily denigrated if they enjoy sex with multiple partners whereas men are effectively elevated. I was never clear on exactly how that was supposed to work.

On top of that, gay marriage was not legal, creating an almost societal push against long-term gay relationships and slightly encouraging them to be more open. I have to wonder if the younger gays will be more relationship-oriented now that marriage is permitted; only time will tell. But I digress. These were simply long-held beliefs at the time rather than conscious thoughts.

I responded that I had a very high sex drive, wondered if a single partner could satisfy it, and that I likely expected some degree of openness. My assumptions about the couple were validated when the woman's face looked shocked and disgusted after my response. Blake was clearly pleased by her reaction; he bragged about the look on her face for years to come. I wasn't consciously aware of either of these things at the time.

I then made sure to clarify that this was only cheating if you lied about it; the most important thing between partners was honesty. I also indicated that it shouldn't be a regular thing and that it is something that comes up a bit later in a relationship once you discover a few needs that you can't satisfy in each other, or your mutual sex lives get slightly boring. It should be permissible to experience a connection with others from time to time, not a regular expectation that this is all you do. I continue to believe that relationships enter a malaise period after a few years. People naturally get bored with the same routine and want some adventure; sometimes you just need to spice things up. The woman's face softened at my responses. They might have made her rethink her initial reaction a bit. I again was not consciously aware of this.

Blake proudly and loudly proclaimed that any relationship he was a part of was to be entirely closed. He put his foot down, so to speak. This actually made me respect him more. He wasn't just a yes man and had no intention of giving me the answers I wanted to hear. Having such a firm opinion made me want to get to know this handsome man. And I considered whether my opinion was childish. A man with morals was intriguing. It projected a certain strength that had been lacking from the previous men I had dated. Blake next painted an unambiguous picture. He had hetero-normative expectations. I got this impression of something we call a white-picket fence lifestyle in the U.S., which idealizes a suburban life with a perfect home and happy family.

This should have immediately been a sign to me that we were not a good match. My primary desires included adventure, learning, exploration and leaving a positive impact on the world somehow. While I occasionally enjoy luxury, it wasn't a focus for my home environment. A comfortable place to sleep, use of my computer, and watching TV was sufficient. Blake clearly valued material comforts far more than I did. He eventually revealed that the opinions he espoused about closed relationships were not real; he never said so directly, but he was clearly manipulating the situation to make me more vulnerable around people who wouldn't understand my perspective.

Thinking the first meeting went well, I was quite happy to consider something more serious, or at least get to know Blake better. I was lonely at the time and had been single for quite a few years. I was ready for something more meaningful in my life and open to considering the idea that my opinion of an open relationship might be wrong.

We parted ways after our first meeting. Not long after getting home, we chatted again on Adam4Adam into the early evening. One thing led to another, and I gave Blake my address, inviting him over that very night. We both jokingly decided that this was our second date, even though it was the same day.

He opened up as the evening progressed, and we had more meaningful conversations about our pasts. Blake talked about his father and blamed him for a lot of the problems in his life. He had always wanted to be in the band while in school, but his father forbade it. He told me he had sent all his military salary back home to his dad to look after. Blake intended to use the money to study music after the military, but his father had spent it all.

That thought obviously shocked and horrified me. What kind of parent steals from their child? I actually thought there were laws in place to prevent this. I sympathized with Blake's predicament, though, as he indicated that his father would become jealous and actively invalidate his achievements anytime he excelled at something. He suggested that his father would not allow his child to outshine him. I comforted Blake as I imagined how difficult that must have made his life.

Blake went on to discuss the horrors he experienced while stationed overseas. When he was transferred stateside, he was sent to Louisiana and ultimately kicked out of the army due to the Don't Ask, Don't Tell policy, which prohibited openly gay individuals from serving in the U.S. military. The general idea was that we were allowed to serve but had to keep our proclivities a closely guarded secret: any form of outing meant discharge from the military. Blake said his sexuality was not the real reason he was kicked out. There was someone who had it out for him for a different reason, which I never learned. In hindsight, there was probably more legitimacy to it than had occurred to me. It seemed like a difficult thing for him to discuss, so I respected what felt like a boundary.

Blake told me that he then went home to upstate N.Y. and that neither parent would take him in due to his sexuality. I can, in retrospect, guess that he was very difficult to be around and that there were other reasons. Afterward, Blake somehow made his way to Chicago, where he became homeless and struggled to get by. Eventually, a priest took him in and taught him to play the organ for the weekly service. He had even been living in the church attic, bringing boys home to sleep with. The priest was aware and considered it Blake's space to do with as he pleased. Eventually, he developed a relationship with someone named Jack.

Blake had learned that his grandmother was dying and needed help to take care of herself; his selfish father was not doing anything for his own mother. So, Blake gave up the life he was building in Chicago and took his partner with him back home to upstate N.Y. They lived together so he could take care of his beloved grandmother. He talked about how hard-nosed she was and that she was quite a nasty person if you crossed her—but she was always sweet and wonderful to Blake who liked this spiteful attitude in a person.

I probably should have clued into the fact that he loved his grandmother because she was mean to people, but his story was so intense and fast paced that I glossed over it then. I also missed the fact that Blake was subtly indicating that he expected me to always be nice to him, while he would expect to be permitted to be spiteful. Potentially, to help distract me from this fact, Blake next reminded me that his grandmother had recently died, and he was planning to use the inheritance to go to school for music. I focused on sympathizing with what he was going through after losing someone close to him rather than his enjoyment of cruelty.

I got a high-level description of his life that sounded true, but Blake left out critical details. He was constantly being victimized by other people and was very good at making you pity him; it was clear he was a lost soul who needed a leg up.

His unique nature and intelligence rang loud and clear. Having been accepted into Mensa myself, the society for people with high IQs, I felt a connection to the inner genius that was already apparent in Blake.

It was a very emotional evening and, by the end of it, I felt incredibly close to him. He exposed vulnerabilities but spoke calmly and rationally about them. He was honest, despite having been through so much. After a few brief hours in his company, I felt he deserved more out of life. I started to care for him; he had real charisma.

I told him it was my birthday the next day, and that I was going tubing along the Esopus in the Catskills with my parents. It is one of the most famous rivers in the Catskills, known for its scenery and challenging whitewater sections.

I didn't mention it, but my father always wanted me to bring my dating partners home because he wanted to feel more connected to my life. Deciding Blake was acceptable to bring along and would satisfy my father's interest in my love life, I invited him to join us. Blake said he would come to be with me, but that he had no desire for adventure or tubing because his time in the military left him wanting peace. I did wonder, again, whether we would be a good match, since my desire for new experiences and adventures of all varieties was compelling.

It was late, and so it made sense for him to stay the night. The next morning, I woke up feeling refreshed and satisfied. Meeting Blake was already a rollercoaster ride, and I felt that I had finally met another gay man who I could forge a meaningful relationship with. He was a diamond in the rough, but I thought he was worth saving and wanted to further pursue the relationship.

I obviously knew he had a lot of issues to work through, but thought he had always had a lot of bad luck and figured he just needed help to turn himself around. I was a bit blindsided by it all. He was an overwhelming man and he made it difficult to fully process all the individual experiences by rapidly moving from intense topic to intense topic. He would cleverly notice negative reactions and distract me with something else.

Before we left to go tubing, I made a quick phone call to ensure my parents didn't mind me bringing this new guy along. They were more than willing to accommodate me on my birthday.

There were more disclosures on our hour-long drive south. I learned that when Blake initially moved to Chicago, he found it difficult to adapt to civilian life. He fell into the wild gay party scene and even supported himself for a while by working as a gay escort; this is how he supported himself prior to meeting the priest. It is fair to say that Blake lived life to the full, without any consideration for his future. Infantry soldiers, in particular, are always pitched onto the front line of battle, into the thick of the action so they feel expendable and expect to die at any time. Their attitude is quite simple: live for today because tomorrow might not come.

I was a little surprised by just how nervous Blake was during the trip. While one certainly expected a few butterflies meeting the parents, his discomfort was palpable. I also knew we had only just met. It felt silly to me. My parents are not judgmental and were always ready and willing to accept me and all my decisions in life. I didn't take heed at the time, but my memories include a look on Blake's face indicating he was quite unhappy in the tube floating down the river.

Blake told me on the way home that he could not swim very well and that while I loved the activity, he reminded me he had had enough adventures in the military to last him a lifetime. His idea of relaxation was anything but an outdoor adventure. I found this droll but didn't say anything and thought we had a great day. My parents thoroughly enjoyed it as well and were happy to meet someone who was part of my life.

Blake told me he wanted to stay over again, and I enjoyed the idea of having a cuddle buddy again for the evening, so I agreed; despite being due at work the next day. In the morning, he didn't want to leave. Instead, he suggested cleaning and organizing my apartment while I was at work. This was slightly discomfiting, having someone in my home without me. It seemed odd that he was so happy to jump in and clean since we weren't living together, and we had only met two days prior. He let it be known that the jumbled state of my apartment was a real bother to him and must have sensed that I would appreciate someone with an organized mindset getting things in order.

Blake had shared so many personal details with me that he had engendered some trust, so I reluctantly agreed. I just wanted him to stay out of the drawers, which were mostly filled with unknown and unorganized paperwork. I was particularly cognizant of these massive unrequested credit-based checks that Discover Card Bank was perpetually sending me; they were hoping I would cash them and go into debt. I never wanted to throw them away until they expired, in case someone else cashed them instead.

"Okay. If you really must clean the apartment, go ahead, but please don't go through any drawers in the living room," I said.

He agreed he would only do the bedroom that day and promised to stay clear of everywhere else.

4. Characters Revealed

Before I continue with the story, I think it's important to share an unusual personality trait I possess. I am very even keeled and for a variety of reasons rarely express, and am frequently unaware of, my emotions. I frequently found my emotions were entirely delayed; in that I would experience them days later rather than as events occurred. My reactions to events also seemed to differ slightly from most other people's, making them hard to predict. It would take me longer to process things, but I think I saw them at a deeper level than most.

It is irrelevant, but I wrote calibration software for color measuring instruments at my first job. One of my coworkers, an older woman, would hammer me for displaying my emotions on my face; she taught me that people would manipulate me if they could tell how I was reacting to events. She taught me to hide them by keeping a dispassionate face at all times.

Another reason I keep my emotions close to my chest is that I received ninja training through my black belt program. One of the lessons was how to sneak directly past people who are looking for you. They taught me to wait until the person was distracted. You would then simply behave as if nothing was out of the ordinary by briskly walking directly past them while looking straight ahead. This technique works over half the time, but frequently the person will realize after twenty seconds or so what happened. I developed an outer shell of perpetual calm so I could sneak should it ever be necessary. Keeping your emotions private from yourself assists with this; best to retain the ability to process them later. My survival did rely on this skill at least once. It comes up much later in our story.

The third reason is that I once hurt some people who attacked me and despite having every right and need to defend myself, I still felt guilty about hurting my would-be victimizers.

The fourth reason is that I think it's inappropriate to behave angrily and that you are better off explaining what is driving your emotions than lashing out. You catch more flies with honey, so to speak. Generally, if you have a good vibe about you, people will oblige to continue it because it is slightly infectious.

One pattern in my life that I noticed while writing this book is that manipulative people will take this as weakness to be exploited. Near the end of the book, we encounter a category of nasty people who take it as a reason to attack you and tear you down.

For these reasons, my general emotional state can be difficult to assess, even for me. There are higher-level emotions happening, but they are just outside my perception. I am not actually aware of them as they occur and process them long after the events that generated them: the effect is that they are delayed. There are lower-level emotions closer to the surface, but even they are generally not expressed, as far as I am aware. Some certainly come through.

Getting back to our main story, I had left Blake at home to clean the bedroom while I had a busy day at work. I came back exhausted and looked forward to a relaxing evening. The bedroom had been organized and deep cleaned. It was lovely and spruced up. Blake had done a good job, and he hadn't simply left with all my most valuable possessions.

But my entire attitude changed when he told me he had also cleaned out all the drawers throughout the apartment and then joked about cashing the Discover checks he had found. It annoyed me that he had broken the first promise he had made.

Most people would likely have reacted in anger, but I held back for reasons I previously mentioned. I reminded Blake that he had promised not to go through my drawers. He played dumb and said he didn't remember saying he would not touch the drawers. My voice was likely rising slightly as I reminded him that he had specifically promised he would avoid them and that it was literally the only thing in the living room he had touched. It made no sense to just go through the drawers. He made me feel like it was my fault; he made it sound like the checks were no big deal and that he had just rearranged the contents of a few drawers.

Now it was my turn to feel rotten. Had it been such a serious thing, after all? I quickly decided it was a big deal and was angry that he had crossed a boundary he had specifically promised to respect. Even with life partners, we should still have our own space and boundaries, and he had stomped all over mine already.

I was about to exclaim something along those lines when he suddenly stepped back slightly, put his hands over his eyes and bowed his head into them as he broke into a flood of excessively loud crying.

"The lawyers talked to me today, and my father gets to decide where I go to school! He says the only thing he'll pay for is a two-year nursing degree at Rural Community College. It's not even a multi building school."

He was bawling and being so dramatic that it overwhelmed me and placed me in a state of shock. Part of me wanted to continue yelling at him about cleaning out the drawers and making jokes about stealing, but on the other hand here was this person who I already cared about and I had never seen anyone so upset. It didn't matter that I'd only just met him. His waves of pain overwhelmed my ability to experience what was justifiable rage.

I briefly considered whether I should focus on Blake being so upset or if I should focus on my anger. What I consider my better side prevailed, and I decided to put that anger aside for the moment. I figured now was not the time, and I could address it later. I moved closer to him to provide comfort.

"Oh, I'm so sorry to hear that. Maybe you can talk to him about it and change his mind? It's not the end of the world. You can figure something out." I put my hand on his shoulder as I looked him in the eyes with concern and love. I tried to hug him.

He stepped back, refusing any form of contact or embrace. His hands became fists, and he pounded them downward, as if a table was there, and angrily shouted, "No... no it is! It's terrible! It's my father doing his absolute best to continually ruin my plans just as he's done for my entire life!"

He seemed to alternate between rage and tears. I was completely shocked by what I was seeing. He only seemed to become louder as he went along and was absolutely wailing with greater and greater levels of intensity. Such minor things: drawers and credit checks. Who cares in the face of decisions that affect your entire life? While I briefly wondered how he worked so diligently on cleaning my bedroom that day if he was this upset and how he was able to be so calm initially, I wasn't able to focus on that for more than a split second. His drama stole my attention and I focused on helping him. The drawers and threats were now completely out of my mind and forgotten about.

"I need money, I need a solid stream of money to accomplish the things I want, and my damned father is constantly standing in the way! He stole my overseas earnings and now has my inheritance too."

I tried to embrace him again while cooing to provide comfort, but he rejected my embrace for a second time by pushing me away and stepping backward. He was now positively wailing as the intensity increased even more. This actually made me pause. I started to block him out so I could think. I realize now I was annoyed, but wasn't aware of it then.

I decided to try to push him toward rationality as I said, "It's okay. I'm sure we can figure something out. You just need to find a different path. Stop and think rationally about it. Maybe a nursing degree isn't such a bad idea; it gives you a reliable income source to help pay for what you really want later. Sometimes it doesn't even matter what you study, just that you have a degree to prove you can see something through."

Blake looked outraged at my suggestion. This was not the response he wanted. His bawling next became deafening, and he started repeating himself. It was so theatrical it was overwhelming my consciousness and invading my ability to think. It carried on for a long time while I continued trying to offer him comfort.

Eventually, I stopped trying to interact and stepped back from the emotional scene unfolding before me. Suddenly, something clicked internally, and I recognized his actions as fake. Real people don't cry like this, getting steadily more dramatic about it, demanding money. The jokes about cashing the Discover checks rang loudly in my head as it occurred to me how calm he was at the start of our conversation.

"These feel like crocodile tears to me. I can tell the difference between real and fake tears. I'd like it if you left. I need some space."

He suddenly stopped crying—like a switch had flipped. No red puffy face, no wet cheeks or any indication his weeping had been real: he was immediately calm.

Looking very serious, he announced, "Okay, I'm going, but I want $300 for cleaning this place up. It would be a real shame if something happened to your car parked on the street outside. Keying is hard to repair." Keying is when someone drags a car key along the side of it, leaving a deep scar in the panel that eventually causes it to rust through.

"You've got to be kidding me?" My eyes were like saucers. This was slightly terrifying as well as confusing.

"Not at all. I spent hours doing all this while you were at work." His eyes followed his hand as he swept it around the room.

I was dumbstruck because I had not asked him to clean in the first place. It was something *he* had wanted to do. He had also only cleaned a single room. I remember getting an estimate from a maid service and for $300, they would have deep cleaned the entire apartment. On top of that, Blake practically earned minimum wage at his job right now. Did he want $75 an hour for something he had offered to do of his own accord?

At this point, I just wanted to get rid of him and to do so, I offered him $100.

He looked me in the eye, smirked briefly, and then strolled out onto the back deck of the apartment. He waited quietly, sitting at the small two-person glass table there. I stood in the living room, stunned and frustrated for about thirty seconds, considering my next move. How do I get rid of this guy? I decided I had no choice but to join him outside.

5. Hooks Penetrate

To my utter astonishment, as soon as I walked out on the deck, Blake started his performance back up again. This time he was wailing and projecting his voice so that my neighbors could hear. I felt embarrassed about what they would think if I crassly shut him down. I was at a total loss for what to do. Standing there in shock for a few moments, I watched him bawl. Somehow embarrassment won and I decided to try comfort him again. This was obviously a mistake.

I stepped forward and sat down next to him as I repeated exactly the same things I had already said, simply rephrased. I patted his hands reassuringly as I spoke. This time, he accepted the comfort and calmed slightly. His performance was no more realistic as he sobbed gently. I slowly brought him back to rationality, and we talked the situation through. Alas, I can't remember what was said but afterward he seemed to melt down and became sweet and caring, loving, and needful of love.

This reignited the feelings he had engendered previously: that I cared for him. It was as simple as that because he had opened up to me about his problems in life. I felt making some allowances due to all his problems and how terrible the world had been to him was in order. I truly wanted to help him. Looking back at this moment, I wish I had realized the world was terrible to him because he was terrible to others. I wish I had screamed the entire situation loudly for all to hear and let my neighbors know this was a violent, manipulative person, and dealt with the fact that some people might have judged me harshly. But I didn't.

We embraced, and with my arm around his shoulders, we strolled into the house together. At this moment, during my emotional weakness, I felt warm and safe with him. But that was not going to last; any indication he was upset went away entirely. He knew he had me on a hook. Once we were out of earshot of the neighbors, he subtly started making demands again. He looked at me with pleading eyes.

"I need someone like you to take care of me, to be there for me permanently." One final sob escaped from him, and he gently laid his right hand on his chest.

My body automatically reeled back, but in my momentarily shocked state, I agreed to this, if only to get him to stop his emotional badgering. I suddenly felt like I had agreed to something and was on the hook for it.

He became much more rational, his eyes smiling and his voice cheerful. He was now working to keep me happy, engaging in something we now call love-bombing. He kept up his intense efforts throughout the evening, and it prevented me from fully considering the situation. During our entire relationship, this would be the only time that Blake cried in front of me. He stayed the night and told me he would get some of his things when I was at work in the morning. He was moving in.

Blake consumed every moment of time I wasn't working, giving me little time to fully consider the situation. He was perfectly pleasant during all of this, keeping me quite happy. He continued organizing the apartment and did a fantastic job. Regardless, I had this nagging doubt for some reason. I actually had forgotten the events that caused me to let him stay. Somehow it was traumatic and slipped my mind, perhaps?

But even dismissing that, there were funny brief comments he would make. Such as calling me "Juden," a term only a German would use unless the person is an anti-Semite and is positively referencing the Holocaust. A few others I can't quite recall. I got the strange impression he was planning to kill me eventually. He implied he could have me murdered if I broke up with him and that I would die if I stayed with him. It is difficult to remember the specifics, but this was a lurking suspicion at the back of mind at the time. Mostly we were enjoying our time together. It was strange little moments that raised the hairs on the back of my neck. Blake was quick to distract me anytime this happened and bring me back to a happier vibe.

After less than a week of his intermittently strange behavior, I privately decided to break up with him but that it would be best not to tell him directly. I would instead just ask for space. This became a long inquisition.

"Listen, I've enjoyed our time together, but I'd appreciate some space to consider this situation. Could you go home for a while?"

"Well, why do you want me to leave?" Blake furrowed his brow, curled up the left side of his top lip and stared at me.

"I just want some time to myself."

After more back and forth, something like an interrogation, he got more information out of me.

"I feel like the sex hasn't been great. You've perhaps been a bit controlling and that we might not be a great match. Something just feels off. I want time to consider this situation more thoroughly."

"So, you're breaking up with me? You need a damned good reason to do that, and I'm not going anywhere unless you have a legitimate reason."

'I just want some space. I'm not necessarily breaking up with you. I just need time to myself for a while. That's enough of a reason."

"No, it's not. You committed to me for life." He settled himself on the couch and folded his arms. "I'm not going anywhere unless you come up with a legitimate reason. You promised to take care of me forever, breaking a vow like that can get you killed."

I stopped and thought, Did he just threaten to kill me if I left him? Do I need specific reasons to break up with someone after a week?

"I'd like some space. I'm just not happy." I wasn't sure what else to say.

We continued like this for a while. He simply refused to leave. I'm not sure if I should have called the cops or physically forced him to leave, but that would have been the only way to actually get rid of him. Somehow, all this eventually left my mind, and we were still together the next day. I simply accepted his continuous presence in my life. He stole every possible bit of attention I had when I was home and was working hard to fulfill my needs and keep me happy, so long as I accepted his presence.

That Sunday, a little over a week after we'd met, he became quite insistent that I join him for his weekly church service so he could demonstrate his musical talent. I now suspect he didn't want me to have time to myself to consider the situation thoroughly or to simply not allow him access to the apartment when he returned. I eventually agreed to tag along and found his music quite lovely despite it being religious music, which wasn't to my liking. Still, a profound and deep soul emanated from his pieces. This was not rote playing. It was quite enchanting.

Eventually, I just moved on from the early suspicions. Even lacking specific concerns, it should have been apparent that we were radically different people with irreconcilable desires in life. He valued material comforts that I enjoyed from time to time but didn't need on a regular basis. My primary desires revolved around adventure, exploration, excitement, video games, my career, and activities. Blake somehow made me consider whether my perspective was childish and if it wasn't time for me to mature into an adult.

The next odd behavior to emerge came during our first shopping trip together. We stuck together initially. I was approving every purchase because I was the one paying and that was a given. He went for the most expensive piece of meat in the store, and I dismissed it with annoyance.

"Oh, we don't need $50 lamb."

There was a single woman within hearing distance, and his reaction was just loud enough for her to hear. It was something about me controlling his purchases; it made me sound abusive. I stood there in a slight state of shock as he walked away after his tantrum. It was like he was a child, and his father would not allow him to purchase the piece of candy he wanted; or perhaps as if we had been together for a long time and I had him on a short leash. I decided this was some kind of childhood trauma and dismissed it as I grabbed a more reasonably priced steak and went to catch up with him.

Life continued, and I forgot about the early bumps. Blake picked up the behavior of a devoted housewife. It was nice having someone take care of the drudgery of life's tasks, and I was keen to spend as much down time with my new partner as possible. Blake encouraged me to drive home at lunchtime so that he could cook a beautiful lunch. It was ready right when I walked in the door, and for forty-five minutes, we would sit down to eat and spend quality time together.

Blake meticulously cleaned and organized the apartment. I thought that was great because it gave us more time to spend together when I was at home. He was taking care of things during the day so we could have fun together in the evenings. I went up to his church several more times so I could hear him play. He was a backup organist rather than a regular figure, but his music was beautiful. It continued to allure me, despite my general unease at being in a church.

He hated the same politicians I did, though in retrospect he was also talking about how much he hated the side I generally supported. I suspect he hated all politicians. Regardless, we both viewed our news as a dual propaganda system (one left, one right) and we both professed progressive values. We would chat for hours about beliefs and the way things should work. He had a bit more of a dictatorial opinion at times and thought punishment should be severe; civilians were too soft and knew nothing of order and discipline. I should have been more wary of his desires for extreme punishment and revenge. I should have seen the stains marking his soul. But then again, Blake was quick to distract me from any negative thoughts that crossed my mind. Like he knew what was on my mind.

After two months of living together, Blake wanted to give up his apartment. He had limited income, and it was a waste of money having two places since we were spending all our time together at mine anyway. I ultimately agreed. After that decision, he had nowhere else to go and no regular income source; we had to make it work. If not, I would at the very least be stuck with him and his emotional instability until he found a new place to live. This was now a semi-permanent arrangement.

Blake wanted to get his cat, Mickey, and possessions from his ex-boyfriend, who lived near his family. The cat was fine because I already had one and figured they could be playmates. I was also curious to meet his family. It was a long drive to where they were, so it made sense to do this all at once.

Meeting them was an odd experience. He had told me about his younger sister and mother. When he finally introduced us, their body language was peculiar. I could not place it at the time, but in retrospect, they were tense and uncomfortable around him. Their eyes and mouths spoke of surprise at my presence. I recall overhearing his sister whispering to her mother, "That man must be a saint."

Blake rapidly interceded and distracted me, so I would not have time to think about it then. Clearer thinking would have allowed me to question why only a saint could date him, and I should have wondered about those ever-so-brief looks of confusion and discomfort. I now recognize them as the kind given by an abuse victim when they are not able to fully divorce themselves from their abuser.

I learned a bit more about Blake. In a joking and nostalgic way, his mother spoke of his horrendous tantrums as a child. She described him sitting on the stairs, screaming at the top of his lungs for hours at a time. She explained how difficult her life had been with her ex-husband. Blake's parents had not been in an ideal relationship and likely should have separated many years before they did. It sounded like the whole thing was doomed from the start. The husband had never wanted to marry in the first place but was forced to by societal expectations when he got her pregnant with Blake. Their religious background probably prevented her from having an abortion.

No doubt this made for a very unhappy arrangement and Blake's father was frequently angry, controlling, and aggressive; with a significant amount of resentment toward this child that trapped him in an unhappy marriage. The way Blake described it, his father abused him both physically and emotionally. His mother had been too afraid to protect her child due to also being the recipient of abuse. It made sense that, to gain any control over his life, Blake had to develop complex plans to trick his father into making the decisions he wanted him to make.

Learning these tactics at a young age likely made them intrinsic to Blake's personality; consequently, he was armed with the tools to manipulate others. After many years of this, his mother became fed up, and they separated—but not until after Blake had run off to the army. I have to wonder if the chaos created by his basic nature had not dramatically escalated any surrounding negativity. Perhaps it was not possible for his mother to consider the situation rationally until the tornado left. Maybe not though, it is impossible for me to know.

I met his father separately; we had dinner with him and his new wife. It was relatively uneventful, and I saw no evidence of anything out of the ordinary. Both seemed like amiable people, but that is not to say he was not a violent bully in his former marriage; especially if he was incredibly unhappy. People can become quite irrational when trapped in an unpleasant situation.

I also met Blake's ex, who seemed like a great guy. He was living with too many cats, including Blake's, and was relieved to be getting rid of Mickey. There was way too much stuff in his cluttered apartment, with boxes and suitcases filling every empty space. Jack was in good spirits the entire time. He was nothing but cordial and friendly: one might wonder if he was wearing a static fake smile to be as conducive as possible to whatever Blake wanted.

There was probably a sense of relief from him about Blake clearing his stuff out, but Jack didn't show it at all. He told us he was waiting until after we left to rearrange the furniture. Jack did not display any outward notion that he was happy to be rid of Blake, other than the static beam on his face and perfectly maintained demeanor.

This suddenly occurred to me. It was like Blake read my mind when he said, "You must be happy to be getting your own space back, right?"

Jack jumped just slightly and said in a slightly squeaky voice, "Oh yes, certainly." He may have sounded slightly nervous.

We stayed the night in Jack's extra bedroom and, after a quick breakfast, grabbed all Blake's stuff, along with Mickey, for the long trip back home. I had rented a truck because neither of us had a large enough car to transport anything substantial. Blake drove his car back, and I drove the U-Haul with his cat in the front beside me.

I probably should have wondered how much Blake had missed his pet when he clearly wanted to be cat free while he was driving. It was my duty to squeak words of welcome and comfort to my new house guest, who was nervous about being in a big, loud truck with a stranger.

Unfortunately, it turned out that my cat hated Mickey, and Mickey didn't like me either. Perhaps being yanked from his home and tossed into a scary truck as an introduction had something to do with it. Mickey pissed into my shoes while I was changing the litter box the next morning, and Blake had to quell fighting between our two animals. He was fairly effective at it by hissing, but soon purchased a spray bottle so he could punish them with jets of water easily. He quite enjoyed them scurrying away anytime he went near the bottle.

6. The Price of Attachment

After a few days of our new arrangement, Blake no longer felt like getting up before noon, and our lovely romantic lunches came to an abrupt end. I had driven home one day to find Blake still sleeping. When I shook him, he rolled onto his side, snuggled in and pulled the cover up to his chin. The cooking novelty had worn off. I obviously found this quite annoying and slightly infuriating. Blake was now lazing about on my dime. I decided everyone was entitled to a bad day.

"I'm starving," he communicated through an enormous yawn. "Couldn't you make one of your delicious gourmet sandwiches?"

On the weekends, I had been cooking sandwiches the way I liked them; by toasting the non-vegetable ingredients from above and below in my toaster oven before finalizing the construction of the sandwich.

However, during the week, it took a good forty minutes to drive home from work, find street parking, gather ingredients, cut vegetables and toast them at just the right speed before putting the final gourmet product together. I then had ten minutes to eat as quickly as possible so I could drive back to work and arrive on time, since I only had an hour. The state was tight with its non-permanent employees. I had to be timely. I proceeded to make lunch with what I can only describe as mild annoyance.

As time passed, it quickly became the expectation that I was going to cook us lunch and my break became more stressful than my job. The eight-minute commute I had to work was now regrettable. This was very annoying, and I tried to broach the topic with Blake, but he wouldn't have it.

'You make much better sandwiches than I do. Can't you do it?'

I'm not exactly sure how, but somehow he made it sound unreasonable for me to expect him to cook me lunch every day. Blake berated me anytime he did not get his way and started to manipulate me, though I didn't realize it at the time because he was generally subtle at this stage.

I began to help clean from time to time, but, according to him, I always did it wrong. I certainly don't meet the stereotype of a typical gay in that my homemaker skills are somewhat lacking. He started to deride my efforts by yelling at me and then giving me step-by-step instructions where I had to do it exactly the way he wanted it done, down to the tiniest detail. He was extremely vindictive whenever I was not up to his standard. Sometimes he had a point, other times both methods of cleaning were equally effective and mine was generally faster and involved fewer toxic chemicals.

Blake started to turn a minor mishap into a round of quick verbal berating and emotional undermining. It seemed almost random and probably was; the randomness makes the victim less able to predict the outcome of the perpetrator's actions. The phrase "making a mountain out of a molehill" could have been written for Blake. I began to feel trepidation about everything I did, and my previous certainty in my decision making was eroded. I started to tread more carefully and became slightly afraid of the consequences of seemingly minor actions.

Any ideas I came up with for activities together were deemed stupid. Only his interests were of value. The things I enjoyed in life eventually became entirely unacceptable, even if I was happy to do them separately. They were a waste of time, though his interests were ultimately of no more value than mine. Because everything had to be done together, we both ultimately had to compromise. We went out to the bars from time to time, with me buying all the drinks. This proved to be expensive and unnecessary, so we ultimately started to spend almost all our time together alone in the apartment.

It was approaching winter and there was finally a nice weekend, perhaps the last one. I hadn't spent time outdoors since my birthday, so I decided to get out while it was still possible.

"Would you like to go on a short hike today? Nothing too intense, just get out into the woods," I suggested.

He screwed up his nose and said, 'That's stupid. Why would I want to put all that effort in just to walk around in a circle and get bitten by disgusting insects?"

"Well, it's nice to be surrounded by serene and beautiful nature; to get away from the noise and bustle of human society. It helps clear your head, and I'm not going to be able to go out soon since winter is approaching. It could be the last opportunity this year. Maybe I can just go out by myself if you don't want to?"

I don't recall exactly what happened, but a minor fight ensued. I'd guess it was about housework, but it didn't actually last very long and wasn't particularly intense. Blake next indicated that I could not go out because things were delicate after our fight, and we needed to patch things up. I reluctantly agreed to stay in, obviously annoyed that I wasn't allowed to do what I wanted. Yet I felt bad about the possibility of leaving him behind. He made me bear guilt about leaving him alone, so we spent the rest of the weekend cuddling and watching TV, which was nice enough. The weather didn't cooperate for future hikes, so it had ultimately been the last opportunity for the year.

Now and then I wanted to play my favorite video game: *Civilization 4*. It was a war strategy game and required constant focus while I was playing because it was online and multiplayer. There were no breaks, or if there were they were negotiated with other players. Having a separate focus and not being available immediately was not acceptable to Blake. If he wanted help with something, he needed it right away, and it would ruin the game because I would lose the "war" by the time I got back to it. My enjoyment of this activity was stupid, according to Blake, and he would deride it at every opportunity.

I became reluctant to go out to eat because Blake had no interest in making reasonable purchases. He wanted an appetizer, multiple rounds of alcohol, the most expensive meal on the menu as well as dessert. I was expected to pay for it all. Generally, I would limit myself to a moderately priced item because I didn't eat a lot anyway and budgeted my limited supply of money. The main course was sufficient. If I tried to cut it back at all, he became kind of coy and persuaded me to be more generous. He was slightly loud and boisterous but just having a good time. I don't recall him manipulating others the way he did during our first meal.

Ultimately, his decadence made our restaurant trips more of an annoyance than a pleasure. We were both decent cooks, so the things we made at home were cheaper and better. We ended up always being alone in the apartment together. I generally enjoyed our time together, so this was perfectly acceptable to me—especially since winter was approaching, and it seemed to be perpetually rainy and cold on the weekend.

The only time we went out was to go grocery shopping. I would describe these excursions as slightly odd, reminiscent of a parent controlling a child's purchases. He would throw minor fits over things he liked that I didn't. It was noon before he got up anyway, so all our meals were together. He started creating crosses to die on and always seemed to do it when female shoppers were around. His ability for dramatic flair was flawless, but I continued to believe his grocery store fits were a product of his childhood. It was difficult to know whether to ignore his outbursts or calm them; I tended to be perplexed by them and stared into space in a state of shock and waited for it to pass.

He did have his intermittent organ job and must have been paying for his apartment somehow until he moved in with me. The idea of him giving up his apartment was that he would have more money to spend on his own things, yet I was still expected to buy the food and make all the other purchases. In retrospect, I wonder if he had simply not been paying rent. He had described the landlord as nightmarish, and if he wasn't getting paid, that would certainly explain the behavior. This started to annoy me, so I encouraged him to find a more permanent work arrangement.

Because he was expected to find work, he was no longer spending time maintaining the apartment and since he was not even getting up until I finished cooking lunch, he only had the afternoon to look for a job. There were no leads, and he was not even preparing to cook before I got home from work.

Dinner steadily became more elaborate and served later in the evening. I wanted to eat sometime between six and seven; eight now and then was acceptable but not preferred. We had been eating at eight and sometimes nine, and it was not comfortable to sleep after such an enormous meal. I would get acid reflux.

I became annoyed with the situation but felt slightly trapped at this point; he had nowhere to go with any ease. I also felt a sense of his revenge tactics and wondered what he would instigate if I just kicked him out. So, I decided to try to push things toward a better state instead and made what seemed like a simple request. "Could you try to get dinner ready before seven most weekdays? I actually didn't even eat much dinner in the past. I need a decent meal for breakfast and lunch. My evening meal can be small and simple. It doesn't really matter what it is. Maybe now and then you can go all out if you really want to."

One might imagine hearing brakes squealing with the look on his face, but he didn't say a thing. I took his silence as agreement. The next day, he had started cooking moments before I walked in the door shortly after five and was moving at a feverish pace. Sounding sarcastic and snide, he said, "I know how important a timely dinner is to you."

I went over and kissed him, and he dismissed me to the living room, which let me relax after a long day at work. There wasn't enough time for my intensive video game, but I could relax, read some news and catch up on things; unwind. He then worked frantically in the kitchen and served dinner promptly at six thirty. It was a simple dinner, just like I had asked for, but it was a decent meal. We relaxed afterward and enjoyed our time together. I liked our quiet, cuddly evenings at home; this is mostly what I wanted as the days got colder and winter approached.

After a week or so he threw together a meal that was very bland and possibly overcooked, but it was timely. I passively accepted it, but certainly internally noted its inferior quality. I didn't want to complain about a meal I had not worked for and figured everyone screwed up now and then.

This seemed to annoy him, so he said, "Don't you think this is really boring and could be better?"

Still not wanting to complain, I said quite passively, "Yea, I suppose it was a bit bland."

The complaint he prompted from me became an excuse to make elaborate meals again. Dinner steadily became later and more complicated. I would put out fine china for our oversized meals served after nine at night on a regular basis.

The massive multicourse meals were delicious and amazing, but way too much food for that time of day and more than I really ever wanted for dinner. I had to pay for all these ingredients I didn't even want in the first place. I did the dishes afterwards, since he cooked, and could not get to bed until one in the morning. Then I would have to get up early to make it to work at eight.

On the one hand, I appreciated having some time to relax after work while he cooked. Plus, now I had enough time to play my game. On the other hand, he needed me at a moment's notice, which always seemed to coincide with the game finally revving up and getting good. By the time I got back to it, I had lost the war once more. I eventually gave up on my favorite game and started doing fewer interesting things.

I tolerated the late meals for a while and even enjoyed them; how could one complain about something so incredible? After a while, the situation caught up with me. I was growing tired of the late meals and wasn't feeling well physically due to lack of sleep and inappropriate eating time. I eventually tried explaining again that the last thing I wanted was a huge meal served at a time I could not eat it.

Why would I want to waste so much food? I was not even hungry at 9:30. I would become ravenous between six and seven, then my appetite went back to sleep. If he wanted to serve a big meal, he had to start the process sooner or make something simpler. It really was not necessary to spend four hours preparing and cooking a meal.

He completely ignored my request. Dinner continued to be extremely late and ridiculously fancy. Our hours consisted of me waiting all evening for dinner to appear and being an intermittent helper available immediately upon his request. Our cuddle time started after 10:30 p.m. and lasted till one in the morning.

7. Promises, Promises

After a while, lack of sleep was really starting to catch up to me. My entire day was one of exhaustion, rushing home to make lunch and then finishing out my day at work without any real break. I was becoming drained. It was affecting my ability to think, which was reducing my productivity and accuracy both at my job and at home; this may have been the reason for the late dinners in the first place. If I couldn't think clearly, I would be easier to control and manipulate. This did not occur to me. I thought it was just his pattern but eventually decided the late meals, while delicious, simply couldn't be sustained. I needed sleep.

Using a tone that I thought expressed care and love, but was also slightly whiney, I said, "Sweety, these late meals are wonderful and delicious, but I really need dinner to be ready by eight at the very latest almost every night. I really need you to make something simpler or start earlier. Even if it means I have to help more. I just need to get more sleep. I have to be up early every day."

He wasn't interested in compromise. "The kitchen is too small for us both to be in here. You'll be in the way. I want to ensure you are having the finest things in life so I can't just make something small and simple, can I? I also can't start earlier. Then when will I have time to look for work? I've been spending all afternoon doing that and haven't found anything yet. You want me to find a job, don't you?"

The start of my reply probably had some annoyance. "Well, you could try getting up in the morning when I do. That way, our schedules align so I can get enough sleep. Then you could start cooking lunch again so I can have a break in the middle of the day. That should give you several hours to look for work, some time to cook and clean and even have some time to relax. Then we can go to sleep by eleven, so we both get enough rest before I need to get up in the morning."

I felt justified with my reasoning and kept the annoyance to the first sentence, I believe. This was another moment where he said nothing, but the look on his face became deadly serious; getting up early was not acceptable to him, and my request was simply ignored.

He still remained in bed until noon, and lunch was still my job.

I eventually had a particularly stressful Friday at work. As I walked in the door, I found Blake busy cooking dinner at a feverish pace. As usual, it appeared that he had started sometime after I opened the door to the building and before I had entered the actual apartment. He did not greet me or stop fussing, acting as if he were immersed in the task. I kissed him on the neck to say hello, and he gave me a brief but very warm verbal greeting.

I went into the bathroom, and when I came out, I said, "I'm going to relax on the couch for a while. It's been a particularly stressful day."

It is almost like I blacked out on whatever it was that happened next. I cannot remember, but he was yelling at me, telling me where to stand in the kitchen and to stay within a few feet of him as he moved around so he did not need to work hard to speak loudly to me while he talked. I woke up from the blackout period and remember acting as if I were on a short invisible leash, terrified of straying from my instructions.

I cannot remember what was so important that he needed to tell me as he frantically cooked dinner and I wondered why he had not started earlier if he was going to be in such a rush to finish it. He had not actually found a job yet, so he only had his intermittent Sunday service he played the organ at. It was not like the apartment was so large that cleaning it was a full-time job.

Eventually, I was standing there uncomfortably, and he didn't want my help or have anything left to say. Somehow, frustration with the situation and the pain in my knees outweighed my terror of more mistreatment.

"My legs hurt. I really need to sit down. Unless you need my help, I'm going to sit down in the living room," I said.

'No, stand here!' He grabbed me by the shoulders and physically put me in a location.

This felt like the last straw. Was I a dog to be controlled like this? "Listen, you can't control me like this. This is ridiculous. My legs hurt. I just want to relax for a little while and not stand here. If you want my help, let me know, but I need to sit for a while."

This started a huge fight that lasted all weekend. The content of words is less important than the incredibly rapid torrent of abuse—it was degrading. He must have sent me off to the living room eventually, and we probably ate dinner either in silence or as he berated me; I truthfully don't remember. Blake's tirade was effective at causing such emotional pain that I can't remember anything other than the overall effect.

By the end of Sunday, I was dizzy from how low I felt, thinking how terrible a person I must be. I was lower than dirt and could not do anything right. I was completely worn down with yelling, berating, and felt that there was never a moment's rest from it. By the time we went to bed, I was too exhausted to do anything but sleep, just to have it start all over again immediately in the morning.

I eagerly went to work on Monday to get away from Blake. Once my head was clear, I decided to escape from this horrible man once and for all. When I got home, I told him he had become emotionally abusive and had crossed too many boundaries.

"I realize you don't have much money and that you have nowhere to go. I want you to take the week to figure out what you are going to do. I'd like you out by Friday, preferably sooner," I said with finality.

This was not taken well at all, and I faced another inquisition; I needed a law degree to argue with him about this. "I'm not happy with you," wasn't a good enough reason. It went on for quite some time and certainly made me angry and fearful. I was brave and held my ground though.

"How can you do this to me? You know I have nowhere else in the world to go. And I've got my cat. Are you prepared to see a helpless animal without a bed?"

The only issue with Mickey was that it didn't like me, and my cat hated Mickey, an uncomfortable situation. Eventually, I agreed to keep his cat for a while since it would be too difficult for him to care for an animal. I could likely find the cat a better home in fairly short order. I stuck to my guns about him, and he agreed to sleep on the couch. That night, I went to bed early and was pretty much a nervous wreck, daring to feel some hope that he might leave.

The next morning, I got to work without much ado and enjoyed a quiet relaxing lunch by myself in a restaurant near my work. I tucked into a scrumptious dish and fantasized about arriving home at the end of the day to see a note from Blake, letting me know he had scoured around and developed a plan for what was next. I really didn't expect him to have left already or to have a full plan in place. Just some things he had done to start. As soon as I got home that evening, I was exasperated to see Blake sitting on the sofa with a serious look on his face. He started with great intensity to try to get me to let him stay. I stared slack jawed, almost amazed at the arguments he was making. They were brilliant.

So, I interceded at one point and inquired, "Wait, what did you do to find a new place to live?"

"Nothing. I thought you wanted me to stay until Friday so we could work this out."

"No. I told you Friday because I didn't want to kick you out with nowhere to go."

His arguments for staying together returned. The content of our discussion was lost in my mind, but it was again overwhelming and infuriating. I eventually stopped him and said, "You need to leave. If you haven't done anything to find a new place by the time I get home from work tomorrow, I may just ask you to leave then."

"But where will I go!?"

I responded incredulously and finally expressed some rage: "That's why I'm giving you until Friday. Take the opportunity." I went into the bedroom and slammed the door. It was only half past seven, and the tiny room was closing in on me. I had nothing to do. At least I was away from Blake.

Wednesday evening was a repeat of Tuesday, but he was even more intense. He still acted like I wanted him there till Friday and had done nothing to consider his next steps. He was quite clearly spending all his time planning how to convince me to keep him. I told him to leave right then, and he silently refused, sitting on the couch and glowering at me.

After several more ignored attempts, I said, "Go now, or I'll call the police."

He smirked and replied, "You smoke weed and there's evidence in the apartment. If you kick me out, I'll report you and they'll arrest you."

This was before any states had legalized the plant. I was obviously frustrated and had no idea what to do. Police and military are a sort of brotherhood, and I figured they would take the soldiers' side in any argument. I also had the general impression that because I was a young male, they were more interested in keeping me under control than protecting me. Young men are typically the source of problems and don't need protection. The police existed to protect housewives and older women from the degenerate young males causing trouble. Not that I had ever threatened anyone.

I additionally felt that I was already being harassed by the local department because they delivered tickets to my car on a regular basis that were clearly outside of regulation. We were required to move the car to the other side of the road for one day a week at 6 p.m. They would ticket you at 5:55 p.m. if you moved it early and 6:05 p.m. if you moved it late. Typically, one was supposed to have a thirty-minute window of opportunity to make the switch. Eventually, these tickets started to pile up, and I never wanted to pay what I regarded as an illegitimate ticket in the first place.

One day, prior to having met Blake, I decided to walk to work and had an eerie feeling, like I was being watched. This happened to be the day my car was sitting on the opposite side of the road. When I returned home from work, knowing I would need to move the car precisely forty-three minutes later without deviation, I found that it had been booted (this meant there was a police device attached to the tire, making it impossible to move). I was unable to do anything about it until the next day, and the person on the phone was quite clear that another cop could come along and ticket the thing minutes after the boot was removed and wouldn't tell me when that would happen. It would obviously be in the middle of the day while I was at work.

I had a few other encounters with the local department that made me distrust them. One had obviously lied to me, and I had reacted angrily to another about having my car towed (again over the ridiculous tickets I'd left unpaid). I had said, "You people are supposed to serve the population and keep us safe, not harass us." The man had an open full-hearted laugh about that statement like this was a funny joke. Yeah, they serve the population. *Hahahaha.* There had even been some reports that they were trying to clean up the department due to generalized corruption.

All of this was in the back of my mind making me feel like I didn't actually get protection from the police department.

I said, "Fine. Take till Friday but find a place to go."

I have no recollection of how, but by the end of Thursday, Blake had convinced me to take him back. He did promise to change his behavior.

"I admit I've stepped over the line sometimes. These were all mistakes, and I can only apologize. But it's not all my fault, you know. You are making too much of little things, mountains out of molehills. It's normal that couples have disagreements, but we don't have to go chucking one another out over trivial things. Please let me stay. You know I can make you happy. I promise I'll try harder."

Somehow Blake was able to make me feel bad about anything he did that displeased me. I felt guilty on the surface, and my fear was being buried deep inside. I accepted his apologies and promises as genuine, so I moved on and decided to accept his traumatizing behavior as a remnant of his turbulent past. He played into this fantasy well.

I eventually remember Blake loving the Saddam Hussein character from South Park. In the cartoon, the Saddam character is highly abusive and manipulative toward his gay bottom partner, Satan. Sadam consistently promised to change and then quickly turned back into his abusive self. He would even sing a repetitive song about being able to change and improve his behavior. Blake would laugh as he sang along with it.

8. The American Dream Surfaces

I have to give Blake his due. He did change and became pleasant again, for a time, anyway. After our argument, he quickly got a job working locally operating an ambulance, which meant he had to get out of bed in the morning and had some money in his pocket at last. But the writing was on the wall, and the signals were all there. He probably had not done anything to look for work until it was actually necessary as a precondition of his continued presence in my life. I shouldn't have let him brush his previous behavior under the rug, but I did.

In late December, about four months after I had met Blake, a new and exciting opportunity arose. A medical technology company in the Midwest contacted me and said they were potentially interested in recruiting me. The offer intrigued me. This was a marvelous opportunity to graduate from small-scale computer systems to larger ones, and it met my primary requirement for a job at the time: that my work would leave a positive impact on the world.

Additionally, the city it was located near was a potential cultural match for me despite being in a generally socially conservative part of the country. The city has a reputation for its progressive and liberal values. It also had enough of a gay scene for me not to feel isolated from the gay community. I had even traveled through it once on a cross-country trip and remembered enjoying my brief visit. On the negative side, it did not have many mountains to climb, as this part of the country is quite flat. It also had brutal winters. I figured upstate New York already had those, so it was nothing new to me.

I had to write an essay for the company and obviously wanted to upgrade my resumé in order to secure the job. Blake helped proofread them both and made some changes, as did some other members of my family. The company flew me out and gave me a series of tests, which I finished with plenty of time to spare. While they were keen to expand their workforce, I also had to pass the interview.

I later learned that the guy who interviewed me had recommended not hiring me. He did so because I was "too confident" in my abilities. I remember having interviewed for a few other positions I had only been mildly interested in, and the most recent interviewer had told me I was too honest about my abilities. He knew the other candidates likely overstated their experience but that it did not matter. He had to hire them over me because they said they had the experience the company needed. I was then overcompensating based on this feedback.

It turns out the company I was interviewing for now did not pay any attention to their interviewers' feedback; they hire entirely based on the test scores. My test scores were extremely high, and I had finished sooner than practically any other candidate. After a few more weeks, they called with a job offer. They also offered me a free short-term apartment on top of moving costs as part of the package. I immediately negotiated a start date several months in advance to avoid traveling on icy roads in the middle of winter.

I was so excited and could not wait to tell Blake that I had been hired. Unsurprisingly, Blake claimed enormous credit for my success in getting the job because he said he proofread my essay and resumé. I accept that my writing skills needed tuning, but I was being hired for my ability to write computer code, not English. Regardless, I was grateful for the help and certainly gave him some credit. It was annoying that he was taking *all* the credit, and I didn't stand for it, insisting it was clear my skills had shone through the process.

Blake gave up his arguments for sole credit and said he was happy to relocate with me, but he wanted a house, not the free apartment I was being offered. He painted a delightful picture; saying he wanted a white picket fence lifestyle and knew how to create a warm, homely environment. He could do that easily, at least when he was rational.

This request slightly annoyed me. It didn't really make sense to jump straight into a house for a job I knew nothing about in a part of the country I was unfamiliar with. What if we purchased something in an unseemly area? This would obviously be easy to do.

I instead argued for the apartment the new company had offered me just minutes away from the job. It would have given us a place to live while we got to know the area and decided where we wanted to live without needing to shop from across the country. Blake's need for a house made the entire relocation complicated when all I had to do was show up and take the free apartment they provided. We could easily decide on a more permanent home, whether it be an apartment or house. There would be three full months to do so and free rent in the meantime.

Blake repeatedly argued for the house and eventually persuaded me to at least consider it. One promise he made was to find work since I really couldn't afford a house at that stage of my life. He arranged two interviews with local churches to be their organist. We had to fly out to look at houses and find him work. We ended up with several realtor appointments scattered across a long weekend and two church interviews on Sunday.

After flying out and viewing the spaces available in the city, we agreed these properties were too expensive. The actual company was a good twenty-minute drive west, which was perfectly fine. My salary was decent but insufficient to afford a house in the city without breaking the budget. The realtor then suggested we look south because it was within a commutable range for work and only forty-five minutes to the city. I agreed to look at these but made it clear once we were in the car that I strongly preferred an apartment.

One house was located in a special, albeit small, community that was charming and historic. The house was very much a 1950s style; it was cute and retro. I loved everything about it, from its curved opaque glass windows at the front of the house to the incredibly retro finished basement, which had a bizarre carpet that was the bright green color of a pool table and had black leopard spots. The fixtures were all built in and had dark stained wood. The rest of the house was more tastefully done, but that basement was like a fun escape from bland.

It was so unique and not cookie cutter in any way. It met all my requirements; the only issues were that it was just slightly above the budget and very much a rural rather than city dwelling. We put down a deposit anyway, but I could not help thinking about the three free months of rent I was turning down. I made it clear that this was to ensure it didn't get purchased in the meantime and that I wanted us to continue to consider an apartment.

Next were Blake's two auditions. We had a good amount of time between them for him to eat and relax a bit. Unfortunately, the first interview lasted way too long. He had to play music for two hours rather than one. Multiple choir ladies pestered him constantly and kept putting different random compositions in front of him to play. It was incredibly stressful and draining for him while I waited in the car with growing concern about timing.

Eventually, Blake texted me and suggested I go to the restaurant to order him something to eat while he finished up. There would barely be time to drive directly to the next church. The food was cold by the time he rushed in, looking exhausted and stressed. We left straight for the next town while he wolfed down his meal. I had already planned our drive, so it wasn't necessary to figure out navigation. I decided to cheer Blake up with a joke.

"Look, this state is shaped like a little hand puppet and the place we're driving to is dead center bottom; it's kind of like the state's asshole."

Blake laughed and agreed. I did not know anything about the place and never spent much time there, but later on I met a coworker who was from the area. He laughed at my joke, agreeing for both location and cultural-based reasons.

We arrived at the second church with no time to spare and I said, "We passed a little restaurant two blocks from here. I'm going to have a beer and maybe a snack while you interview. I really don't want to sit in the car for another two hours or however long it takes."

"But you can't do that. The church has invited you in as well. They probably want to know more about us. It would be rude to turn them down."

He could have warned me about that—and maybe he didn't so that I wouldn't be adequately prepared. I was nervous and had *not* prepared to be part of an interview. I was raised without any formal religion, identified as slightly more Jewish than Christian, and being in churches made me uncomfortable, even without a job on the line. It seemed strange, but I got out of the car to head into church. Oh boy.

As we entered, a curious sight greeted us. The choir was composed entirely of middle-aged white ladies, just what you would expect in a medium-sized town in a rural part of the state. The pastor, meanwhile, definitely looked like he had African ancestry. My eyes lit up as this arrangement began to fascinate me. I was no longer put off by being forced to participate. I now wondered what lessons he was here to teach and about the nature of the people who were willing to learn from him. What a wonderful little church.

The pastor greeted us cordially and then asked me if I would like to speak to him in his office while the ladies interviewed Blake. I told him I was surprised he had asked me in and offered to hang out at the restaurant/bar around the corner. The suggestion surprised the pastor. I was not sure if the idea of a bar put him off, but he said he felt obligated to entertain me and that he was relieved to have time to continue his own work.

In the end, Blake got me to agree to the house purchase. It was what he wanted, and he was so persuasive. We already had one in hand, making it easier to simply proceed with it.

We waited for the phone calls and emails from the interviews Blake had attended, but unfortunately, nothing materialized. Here we were, moving cross-country, and he did not have a job. We tried to stay positive, believing that something would turn up when we arrived. I wondered, in retrospect, if the second pastor had hoped to enlighten his flock by employing a respectable gay couple and if I had failed that test by mentioning the bar. I also wondered if I could have gotten that pastor to hire Blake by staying. It turned out better that he was not successful. The logistics would have been difficult for us. His job would have been an hour-long drive from our new house and in the opposite direction from my work.

While things weren't exactly as I would have wanted, they were within reason and certainly acceptable. Meanwhile, our life together had normalized; I thought Blake's issues had been worked through and that he had accepted his new life with me wholeheartedly and honestly. Blake's ambulance job meant he had money in his pocket for his own expenses. He was on my schedule, and our time together in the evening was exactly as it should be: a reasonably timed dinner with me helping out with some cooking and cleaning. We had a few hours afterward to cuddle and were enjoying our time together. Blake would disappear to play the organ from time to time, which gave me an opportunity to enjoy my online war game or just have time to myself.

The only issue that emerged was that it was a nightmare coordinating the move between Blake and my new human resources (HR) department because he needed to be in control. I eventually gave the entire process up to him. One HR lady later described him as "very intense." A politely phrased understatement. Nevertheless, I always appreciated Blake's ability to take on an enormous, complex task and implement it forcefully, albeit a little too forcefully at times. This was how I felt then, anyway.

Eventually, I decided Blake had simply avoided easy non-optimal solutions and planned for too many eventualities, making what could be extremely simple into a monumental task. I always figured if something went wrong with your straightforward plan, that you correct it organically as you go. Now and then you land somewhere unexpected, or things are slightly less than ideal for a while, but tolerable until a solution is found.

Life had been fairly good to me in general and this strategy had worked well. For Blake, it was a different story; he had a catastrophic background. I chalked it up to his difficult past and figured that his army training also contributed. Soldiers have to plan for every eventuality upfront because it might not be possible to reliably contact other groups and make new plans ad hoc without the enemy overhearing. On the other hand, it may have been because it was my money being spent, and he didn't need to worry about earning it.

I trusted him and didn't worry about these things, so our first winter together generally progressed nicely. Blake's tantrums had completely subsided at this point, and he was dealing with all the move-related coordination with a laser-like focus. My memory of his early tantrums faded, and I thought we had worked through them. Deep down, I knew he had quite severe problems. He could be a twisted individual at times, but I somehow became convinced he had a profound, beautiful soul that needed help to emerge.

I could continue to help him work through his problems so the diamond in the rough I saw at the beginning could shine. The interests he had derided were probably a relic of childhood, and we could build a pleasant life together. Maybe a 1950s housewife is exactly what I needed all along to take care of me.

I would never have suspected what would happen next, but it probably should have been obvious.

9. Target Isolation

About two days before we were due to leave, Blake suddenly changed from having an abundance of excitement about the move to having an anxiety attack about it. This seriously freaked me out; I couldn't understand how somebody who had been 100% behind the relocation for months could immediately and suddenly be so negative about it out of nowhere.

"What's brought this sudden anxiety attack about the move on?" I asked Blake as he paced the living room floor.

"I need assurances if I'm going to move cross-country with you."

"And what about us? We're starting a life together. A new chapter in the book. We're practically set to leave."

"I'm scared that you won't need me or want me once I'm so far from home. What if things go wrong between us? And I don't have a job yet. I feel so vulnerable without my own money, without the freedom to—"

I put my hand up, stopping him mid-sentence, and decided to calm his fears. "If things don't work out between us, I can help you move back to New York if you want. I can send you to your hometown or—"

He interrupted me, exclaiming, "What!? Why would I ever want to go back there? I'm not going back to that tiny, boring place!"

Gasping slightly, I continued, "Well, wherever. If we break up, I'll help you get somewhere else you want to be. I won't just abandon you and kick you out; we'll figure out the next stages of your life together as long as you're being reasonable. I also know that setting up a house is a colossal task in and of itself. I'll avoid pressuring you to find work immediately and let you focus on building our new home. Money is going to be tight though. I'll eventually need you to find something."

This seemed reasonable to me as he was moving because of my job, and it was not exactly a target destination for most gay men. Blake looked like he had won something, but this was my immediate offer to him—one I was happy to provide. It all made sense under the circumstances.

There were legitimate concerns in his next questions, ones that we should have discussed calmly over the course of the previous three months. I had my typical reaction to things and kept an outward calm; inwardly, though, I was in turmoil. Blake would share a concern, and I would address it or come up with a good reason why it was silly to worry about in the first place. I was silently panicking because it would be very difficult to pivot and move alone with so little time remaining.

I eventually halted him mid-sentence, "Listen, I don't see why you need to make such complex plans or for me to give you all of these crazy reassurances all of sudden. There are legitimate concerns baked into all of this, but we should have discussed these things calmly over the course of the last few months, not suddenly become scared of them at the last minute. I know life has not been kind to you in the past, but certainly by now you must realize that I'm not the type to just throw someone to the wolves. I'm asking you to trust me."

I put my hand on his cheek and looked him in the eyes. "I won't just abandon you if things don't work out. I've already told you; I'll help you move on if we split, but I want us to make a life together. All you need to do is believe in me and work diligently towards a shared happiness."

Blake pulled back, looking angry. He next retorted with a list of demands that related to purchases he required as a prerequisite for moving. The initial ones weren't so bad, and I agreed to them. But I started to get slightly reticent as the costs quickly added up. The next thing he asked for was a new car, which I rejected as infeasible and unnecessary. He smiled anyway, having won most of what he wanted and said, "Fine, but I need an organ instead."

I almost choked at this ludicrous demand and must have sounded quite annoyed by now. "What? I couldn't afford one of those even if I wasn't stretching myself thin to purchase a house. Aren't they thousands of dollars at the very least? I don't have that kind of money."

Sounding like a dreamer, he said, "Oh, but I found one! It's only $5,000. Way below the general cost because it doesn't actually work right now. Your company can pay to move it and I'll fix it after we arrive. I know I can."

I replied, 'What? Literally every last penny I have saved is going to the down payment for the house. There's absolutely no way I could afford that right now and you have nothing to contribute yourself. Even if I could, why would this company that doesn't even know me yet pay to move something that probably weighs over a ton across half the country when we don't even own it yet? They pay by weight and it would probably cost $5,000 in and of itself. They will absolutely not approve that at the very last second before the move. They would likely fire me on the spot for having the audacity to ask in the first place.'

He had an answer ready. "Fine, then I want one shortly after we arrive."

Still sounding annoyed and growing tired of his ludicrous requests, I once more clarified the situation by saying, "No. The budget is at the absolute maximum and there will be large costs just setting up the house. I'm not even sure how I am going to afford those let alone an organ on top of all the other things you just made me agree to buy. Perhaps you can find a local church that will let you use theirs or something. I have no problem with you taking some time off to practice but where do you think I am going to come up with thousands of dollars to purchase a musical instrument? Like I said already, every last penny I have is going to the house you insisted we buy, and we are barely going to squeak through the purchase process itself. What if something major breaks? We need money on hand to repair things. If you don't fix some problems immediately, the costs only get higher. We need an emergency fund, not a bunch of new toys."

Blake said, "But an organ! Just imagine it... your own private concerts. I need an organ."

This went back and forth a few times, and I kept rejecting it, holding my ground. Eventually, he started a long tirade. I took a step back internally by ignoring what he was saying so I could think. I noticed the pattern of me agreeing to one thing, ending in him requesting another. My traumatic memories of our first few months together emerged. All the progress I thought we had made over the last few months was gone. This was the exact same behavior he had demonstrated before I failed to break up with him last time. I started to consider whether I should move alone and started planning that in the back of my mind.

With finality, I eventually interrupted him and said, "No. Absolutely not. No organ. It can't be done."

He looked me up and down while grimacing, "You expect me to move halfway across the country for your job? You need to buy me this organ."

"Okay, never mind, I guess," I said. "I'll make the move on my own." I shrugged my shoulders and turned my back to him while I considered how I was going to do this all alone.

"But where will I go?" he stumbled backward onto the sofa.

There were a few moments of silence while I thought with my back turned so I didn't have to look at him. I quickly realized that I didn't even need a plan; I could just take the free apartment. Exactly what I would have done in the first place if Blake hadn't been involved in my life. The company probably had plenty of apartments anyway. They had basically implied that they were rapidly growing and hiring at a frantic rate. Finding a year-long lease would be easy after I arrived and started living in the area. That wasn't even a real concern.

I next realized that I didn't actually want to live in the small town anyway and would likely be a lot happier in the city than the rural lifestyle that Blake had chosen. On top of that, I would soon be a thousand miles away. There was nothing he could do to me. His threats would be almost impossible to engender with his financial instability and that kind of distance. This quiet, mostly suppressed fear he had instigated in me through his intermittent angst attacks and randomized bullying felt slightly calmed.

I carefully considered how to break this to Blake and realized that I was expected to give him a plan for his life as well. I eventually said, "Well, I have ten days left on my lease. You can crash here while you look for a place and technically you haven't quit your ambulance job yet. There's your solution."

Looking aghast, he sat in silence while we both looked at each other. I became slightly concerned he might trash the apartment as revenge, but I knew that landlords rarely return the deposit anyway and decided that I didn't mind eating the cost of ten days' rent. It was nothing in comparison to the ridiculous demands Blake had been making. Ultimately, the landlord refused to refund me the last ten days of that month's rent anyway, as he had previously promised.

After perhaps a minute, Blake said, "Yeah? And what are you going to do?'

I already had my answer ready. "We haven't finalized the purchase of the house. I can just forgo the down payment and take the free apartment."

I felt a sense of relief with these words. A burden was being lifted. Was I suddenly freed of this insanity? But alas, once I said that, a strange thing happened. Blake realized that I was no longer backed into a corner with no way to handle myself without him. He grasped that we were talking about a serious separation and didn't want to have to support himself.

So, he completely flipped the previous script. Suddenly, he became reasonable and practical, begging me to stay with him. Separation was no valid option; he loved me so much, and now he was telling me he would walk to the end of the earth for me. An organ was unnecessary, as was the previous list of less onerous demands as he gave them up one by one. I made it clear that I was still willing to help him set up a new life if we didn't work out. It was quite an amazing transformation. Only two minutes earlier, he needed more and more financial promises to be convinced to go. Now it was anything I wanted so he could come along.

In truth, I'm not sure how he convinced me to stay with him. It should have been clear to me that he would be a relentless bully anytime he felt he could get away with it. I also should have realized that his list of demands was well thought out and not the result of a sudden anxiety attack. He had purposefully planned to drop them at the last minute so I would have no choice but to agree to them lock stock. I was so close to relocating on my own that day. There were so many of these *Sliding Doors* moments like in the movie with Gwyneth Paltrow. What direction would my life have taken if I had made the break and gone on my own? But I chose to stay with Blake, because once again, his powers of persuasion and the promises he made convinced me to make the move with him instead of alone.

The next day, the movers came and grabbed all our boxes; professionally packing the inexpensive but deeply personal and beautiful art I had collected over the years on my travels and wandering around yard sales.

I remember trading someone an extra cable of some kind for this beautiful green leaf piece that always gave me a sense of peace. I had purchased a charming Asian work that was potentially worth hundreds for only $50 at a yard sale. My father had bought me a 400-year-old Tibetan padlock; it was similar to a master lock but larger and sturdier with keys that had symbols for enlightenment engraved into them. I also had several other paintings that depicted enlightenment: a North American man-wolf my aunt had given me, a Peruvian painting of a pair of hands holding the world up with strange little UFOs my grandmother had presented me with, as well as a few other pieces of art that had emotional significance. I felt immense pride in my collection as the movers carefully packed.

When we left, I suspect we both dreamed of a fresh start, but Blake probably had a different end goal in mind. I had no love for the idea of a small town but committed myself to building a home in this unique little village.

We loaded separate vehicles full of our possessions and drove cross-country because the movers would arrive well after us, and we needed some things before that happened. Blake insisted I take both cats, despite the fact that they would fight in such a small space. I had to deal with them while I drove; we stopped for a while, and I wanted to give him one, but to my annoyance he again refused. I remember it being a decent drive otherwise. We stopped about halfway in Ohio to visit my aunt and grandmother.

It was fairly uneventful except that my aunt had two cats, and there was some amusing drama. The first cat was a giant sweetheart and developed a crush on mine. He was stalking her, and she eventually became annoyed, spraying some kind of urine-fecal mixture all over the hardwood floor to drive him away. The look on the lover-boy's face was not one of derision but rather, "Wow! What a woman!" Fortunately, it was easy to clean off the wood. From here on, Blake nicknamed my cat Ass-pee; which he said with great affection in his voice.

My aunt's other cat was more of a psychopath. It tried bullying my cat and almost killed her, but she was quick-witted and kept a good eye on him from there on in, ensuring to place herself in strategic locations to remain safe. Psycho-cat instead picked on Mickey, who was clearly a beta and had no idea how to deal with violent bullying. Poor little guy needed constant attention, and we ended up locking them both in the bedroom to keep them safe.

We left after a few days and stayed in a small Chicago hotel room for a night. We enjoyed some time in the city where Blake had been homeless. He took me to a dance club I would eventually decide was one of my favorites: Berlin. They never seemed to have an off night and always had amazing music.

We finished up our drive, arriving a week or two before I was due to begin work. The idea was that we could move in before my job started, but the bank had other ideas. There would be no closing on the house until a week after I began. We ended up renting the space from the current owner in the meantime.

The cats were initially fighting, but Blake quickly quelled them with jets of water: something he clearly enjoyed. Eventually, they started to avoid each other in the large house. We had a huge living room with big bay windows overlooking a small three-season porch we could smoke on comfortably in the winter. There was a nice half-wall separating it from the large kitchen, which had more counter space than I'd ever had before. It also had plenty of cupboards as well as a dishwasher and garbage disposal.

There was a decent-sized dining room separating the kitchen from the aforementioned porch. It overlooked a three-tiered backyard that would have plenty of space for a vegetable garden. There were three large trees occupying the middle tier as well as a small forest giving us privacy from the neighbors behind us and a place for small animals to play. The living room and kitchen opened up to a shared hallway that led to three bedrooms, a driveway with a disconnected garage and stairs that led down into our finished basement that practically gave us a second kitchen-less small apartment. It had my computer set up and an extra futon providing a fourth room for someone to sleep. It was all replete with finished wood and an absolute beauty of a well thought out and designed home without having the standardized factory feeling that modern homes have.

There were wonderful, thick, clouded glass windows that replaced the outer corner of each of the front bedrooms. They were perhaps eight feet in length and went from floor to ceiling; providing amazing, slightly dimmed light for the rooms while preserving utter privacy from whatever was happening on the very quiet street outside. The front yard was fairly small. It perhaps had room for a few flowers, though. The side yards were also small, and the larger one had a disgustingly ugly tiny tree growing in it. We were marveling at its audacity to be so hideous when the neighbors noticed us and laughed. They assured us that it was a hydrangea and flowered beautifully for most of the summer. They clearly didn't mind living next to a gay couple and welcomed us to the neighborhood.

Blake kept busy, diligently setting up our home and maintaining his sweet character. He was, in fact, creating a wonderful, warm and homely environment filled with care and love. Meanwhile, I started work and threw myself into my new job. There was a lot to learn and dozens of colleagues to build relationships with. I was also busy with finalizing the formalities of the purchase of the house and nervous something would go wrong.

I certainly had a nagging doubt. Even though I liked the place, I knew deep down it was not a choice I would make willingly. Blake and I were polar opposites; while he had the housewife fantasy with an idealized dream of the perfect happy home, I felt trapped in an area that was alien to me. I longed for the city, having access to the bars, clubs, and restaurants it presented. There was even a small, beautiful mountain north of the city that had a lovely lake. It was far away from our home, south of that city.

Even so, I appreciated the homemaker in my life who took care of the household environment more than I thought possible. Maybe this was okay. I decided to ignore the negative feelings and embraced our generally happy life together. I must have had butterflies. New things are always scary.

I finalized the purchase of the house and sealed my fate. Little did I know, but all the intensity I had experienced from Blake would only magnify now that we were entirely in one world together.

Blake next suggested I change my cellphone number. I thought it was a strange request, but he became insistent and said he wanted to distance himself from "all those assholes in New York."

He had every right to his opinions, but I certainly had the opposite feeling. I had some good friends back home. If I knew any jerks, they would never call anyway. He swamped me with his aggressive persistence and would not take no for an answer. After days of unrelenting barrage, I surrendered.

I later realized it was a tactic to cut me off from all the old friends who I knew and loved. Blake created a situation in which it was hard to get rid of him, isolating his target and then steadily controlling it, controlling me.

10. The Gilded Cage

Blake rapidly became insistent about funny little things. While my expectations were subtly and briefly complied with, they were quickly forgotten. His, meanwhile, were not to be ignored for any reason. An example is morning coffee. I am unable to have any before a large breakfast, as it makes me jittery. For him, it suddenly became essential for it to be prepared before he woke up and ready at the instant he did. This never happened at a consistent time, so I had to be able to predict his awakening or let it sit on the burner, potentially for hours. Ensuring it was ready wasn't such an unreasonable demand, so I generally complied, and he didn't seem to mind the gross old, burned coffee on days he slept in anyway.

One morning, my parents called quite early, and we were on the phone for a long time. This woke Blake up a bit earlier than expected, and I had yet to prepare his morning joe. With my parents still listening, he starts screaming, "Why isn't there any god damned coffee? You have to make me coffee in the morning!"

My not so unreasonable reply was, "I'm sorry, my parents called; could you make it yourself today? I am in the middle of a conversation here."

My mother next recalls him screaming at me for several minutes, with them still listening. I eventually just hung up so I could make him coffee. Most of his demands were fairly minor like this, but I started to feel like his servant at times. Meanwhile, I let him manage the house as he pleased. He did a very good job of it, making a perfect home.

It was obviously a lot of work, and there are always tools available to make things easier. Unfortunately, they all cost money, and I was relatively tapped straight away. This was of little importance to Blake, who didn't mind me going into debt and was quick to level accusations of financial abuse if I said no. We would have frequent conversations where he wouldn't let go until I agreed to buy some new fancy toy to make his life easier. I would eventually have to give in and purchase whatever it was. His requests were unreasonable, given my financial condition after purchasing a new home.

We both wanted a garden, and I was happy to be the primary planter. This was good because Blake had a black thumb while I had a natural ability to care for plants and enjoyed the work. I planted a beautiful vegetable garden and gigantic perennial Hibiscus flowers that produced dinner plate–sized crimson red flowers throughout August in the front garden as well as several beds of annuals. Being rural had its advantages, and I remember seeing a rabbit watch us while I planted the vegetables; it respected our space and left the garden alone that first year. I remember doves nesting on our porch and homemade coleslaw from Kohlrabi I had grown.

Blake was even willing to join me on the occasional outing, though local walks were hardly the isolated woods I most enjoyed. This state had few of those. It was all pretty rolling farm hills without a mountain to be had, other than one that was a respectful distance from where we lived. The surrounding community was, in and of itself, quite interesting to explore, with its unique and highly specific cultural heritage that in no way reminded me of the strip malls back home.

As our first summer together progressed, the house was beginning to take shape. There was just one component missing.

Sex!

It had not stopped altogether, but Blake never let me initiate sex and only seemed to be in the mood at the strangest moments. Like when he was drunk or if I bought him something nice. It felt almost like a contract, an obligation. I started to feel like a John (someone who uses a prostitute). From having a very active sex life prior to making the move, now Blake rarely wanted any intimacy. I was a normal young man with needs. I could do nothing about my hormones and testosterone, the influences, cultural factors, and personal experiences that all played a part in my high sex drive.

I tried to convince myself that the sex was not so important and yet I missed it. We would cuddle and spend all our time together when I got home from work, watching TV and having long conversations about the state of the world. We seemed to agree about the state of things most of the time. When our opinions differed, I even felt like my worldview had expanded to a degree.

We tried kinky play at some point to spice things up. When I was in charge, he got furious about things we had specifically discussed ahead of time, and it took days to calm him down. When we reversed the role play and he was in charge, he took complete control and immediately crossed every limit we had set together. He would emerge from our BDSM sex session with a smile on his face, clearly satisfied, while I voiced my displeasure that he had crossed boundaries as soon as I was all tied up. My concerns were dismissed; he could do no wrong. It should have been obvious to me he wanted to be in complete control, and nobody was going to step in his way, in the bedroom, or anywhere else. I instead developed a bit of depression about the state of our sex life. If I expressed it, Blake would deride sex as unimportant and make me feel guilty for having needs. This caused me to retreat further into myself.

Like most couples, we argued a lot of the time about nothing of any significance. Rather than a row where we would agree to disagree after a few minutes, Blake would start to get aggressive, angry, and unreasonable. The rows steadily got longer, hours instead of minutes. Eventually, I would join the fray vociferously as well. It probably took about forty minutes of barrage before I joined a shouting match. Even when I agreed with his side of the argument or pointed out the reasons his argument made no sense in the first place, he would start all over again almost immediately but with greater rage and urgency.

This is typically when my own frustrations would break through my calm exterior, and I would raise my voice in reply or say something that would otherwise have been inappropriate. The fight would then become about my horrible statement and how terribly I treated him. He would break me down, and I would ultimately give in to him almost every time. A discussion of his own inappropriate actions was never tolerated. He would simply ignore such complaints and focus on my reactions to him.

Blake once again started to deride all my interests and became upset if I wanted to do anything separately from him, even if it was something that he had no interest in. He would take umbrage at something else in the process and then berate me until we were fighting about a different subject entirely. Then things were too delicate for us to do something on our own right now. We had to patch things up, right? I eventually gave up having my own interests.

On top of that, the bills for sewage, electricity, gas and water were dropping through the letterbox. To say money was tight was an understatement, especially to the extent Blake spent it. The sewage bill was by far the largest. For some reason each unit of sewage had cost something like twenty times each unit of water.

Blake wanted to water the lawn, so that it was always green and perfect. He was unwilling to reduce our water usage.

The water company let us pay five dollars a month to read the outside usage of water and subtract it from the sewage bill, but Blake refused to go along with that for reasons I could not comprehend. It was morally unacceptable to pay the extra fee to reduce your total bill. I could not understand but did not want to deal with fighting him about it. So we paid hundreds instead.

Blake had never been good at earning money, only spending it; this was becoming a real bugbear for me and caused many of our arguments. I eventually just gave him my credit card and told him to buy what he needed because I could no longer deal with the arguing. Then we would go to the grocery store, and he would act like I was going to throw a fit if he bought some basic food item that he wanted.

He would ask, "Do you want grapefruit?" and I would say, "I don't like grapefruit."

Then suddenly he would throw a fit. "You know I need breakfast too! I get to eat!"

I would be stunned and say, "Um yea, sure you get to eat. Yea, you can have grapefruit. Grapefruit isn't expensive. I just don't like it myself. You asked if *I* wanted grapefruit."

By the time I finished talking, he had stormed off. I remember picking the grapefruit up and wandering around to find him; he was in a different section of the store. He refused to let me buy the grapefruit, and I abandoned it on a random shelf. Then, later, he complained about having to skip breakfast.

"Then buy yourself food for breakfast; yes, you absolutely get to eat. You can eat breakfast and lunch. You have my credit card after all, don't you?"

The idea that he could go out and make large purchases for the house but not purchase relatively cheap food items for himself seemed preposterous to me. I could not understand his logic. Now I have a better understanding, though: it was about creating the appearance of abuse for others. There is an old 1990s British TV show called *Keeping Up Appearances*. The main character is a standard woman who lives a standard life and lets her house and herself become a mess, in private, from time to time. It would feature her going to ridiculous lengths to clean things up and make them prim and perfect for very brief interactions with the postman; wouldn't want him to see your house a mess and judge you, after all. Blake very much knew how to keep up appearances and control them to appear however he wanted.

We were different in so many ways. While Blake wanted the prestigious lifestyle such as fine bone china dining sets, I was more interested in a decent dinner and could not have cared less about what plate I ate from. Fortunately, there was a very nice antique shop in town that sold 1950s glass and serving plates at a ridiculously low price. Things you would pay an arm and a leg for in a big city, you could buy here for a dollar. I did not mind purchasing those, but preferred dishes you could put in the dishwasher. I wanted things to be quick and easy so I could enjoy my free time rather than spending it cooking and cleaning. Once again, Blake would spend hours preparing overly elaborate meals. We would frequently finish eating after ten o'clock.

But even then, he threw that back in my face. He told me he was doing it for me because he wanted to see me enjoy the finer things in life. It was of no importance that it was things he wanted rather than me. Blake was clearly done setting up our new home, but still had no interest in finding work. He seemed content with his housewife role, albeit the aggrieved one he positioned himself to be.

I was hard at work during this entire time, acclimating to a large and ridiculously complex computer system that had been upgraded a bit at a time for decades without ever being re-written from the ground up.

Other tech companies I had worked for describe something called tech debt, things you had to carry around with you all the time because someone out there was relying on it. You had to invest time to simplify things, or you would perpetually be maintaining more and more as well as screwing things up because the system had grown too complicated. Other companies had some extra weight to lug around. This place had a giant ten-ton metal ball shackled to its legs as it blithely rushed forward into the future.

The discussion over the organ cropped up again in early fall, just a little over a year after we met. I was concerned that I was at my financial limit because of the house, but he went on and on and on for weeks, so I eventually agreed.

I paid $4,500 for it, tossing every penny I'd managed to save up as an emergency fund since the purchase of the house. We now had to get it into our basement somehow. There was a staircase that curved at 90 degrees. Blake stood in front, and I stood behind, trying to pull it upward to reduce the weight pushing him downward. It was ridiculously heavy, and our tactics turned out to be impossible, so in a strange karma moment, we lost control, and the weight of the organ nearly crushed him against the wall where the stairs turned. He managed to move out of the way just in time. That left a hole in the wall. We let it slide down on its own the rest of the way. Blake was uninjured, but he had to make several repairs to the damaged instrument.

Although there was some resentment and bitterness on my part about the cost of the purchase, I must confess that Blake played the most beautiful music. I truly never enjoyed the organ other than when he played. He composed music that was beyond comparison to anything I had ever heard in my entire life, but he refused to let me record it. I adored listening to him play as I relaxed in the evening. This gave me a chance to play my video games while he kept busy making lovely music.

Looking back on Blake's musical talent, I wish he could have found a way to share his gift and make real money because he was certainly good enough. I had even suggested he apply at my work because they had an organist play once a month before a company-wide staff meeting. He was adamantly opposed because he knew church music rather than theater music. Based on my listening, he could have played whatever music he wanted, and the company would have adored it.

To make financial matters even worse, the furnace went out shortly after I purchased the organ and there was no choice but to replace it immediately. The financial buffer I had built up for just such a catastrophe was already spent so I had to go several thousand dollars into debt or risk the pipes freezing.

My relatives came for a few visits, and Blake was always a dream when they were around. He must have been antsy for them to leave though. There was a smudge on the windshield as I was driving them all to the airport and I didn't bother cleaning it up as it wasn't bothering me. Blake decided to intensely berate me about it right in front of my family. Many years later, my relatives let me know that they started having doubts about our relationship after seeing this behavior. No one said anything to me at the time, they wanted to support my decisions and did not want to risk alienation from me by rejecting the man I had chosen to spend my life with.

Eventually, our sex life became almost non-existent, once a month at the most, and I knew I wanted out. I had not yet reached thirty years of age and I had needs. This was not how I viewed a long-term relationship taking shape. We should at least be having decent sex early on, shouldn't we? The long malaise of a relationship is not supposed to set in for several years at least.

I seemed unable to make plans, and if I tried to participate in planning with Blake, things always got very confusing. I could never keep track of what was happening next and frequently I received inaccurate information only to be called stupid for relaying what he had told me back to him; suddenly the plan had changed or had components I wasn't made aware of. I went from having certainty in life decisions, both important ones and entertainment-based ones, to never being sure what was going to happen next. I learned to just go along with whatever Blake was planning to avoid being castigated for stupidity or confusion as to what was happening. This generally kept him happy and allowed me some degree of my steadily eroding sanity and self-respect.

On top of that, I was losing my mind with the stupidity of things Blake would become incredibly upset about. Minor issues related to housework, desires I had that he didn't approve of, reacting to it all by becoming withdrawn. Anything was up for grabs. There were many times where something I had done would suddenly become unacceptable and warrant hours of angry degradation. I started to question whether it was right that we stayed together. I genuinely felt we would both be happier if we separated, but Blake would have none of it. Any time I raised concerns about our relationship, Blake would spend at least four hours destroying my mental and emotional state using what I can only describe as interrogation tactics. By the end, I was prepared to do anything to get it to stop.

I tried to broach the topic of potentially separating with him a few times. I told him that there was clearly something wrong with the way he was treating me and with our level of intimacy. We wanted different things in life. He would always turn my words on their head, talking and talking, berating and persuading until I relented; otherwise, he wouldn't stop. I would eventually become exasperated, sit quietly taking his abuse and wait for it to pass, only to give into every demand and any hope of separation.

Looking back, the suicide threats were the worst. He told me on more than one occasion that this was his last shot at life and if we separated, he was going to kill himself. Did I believe him? Probably. I think Blake was capable of almost anything and because I was so emotionally attached to him, I would take him back or agree that I had changed my mind and he could stay. And then, for a while, the kind and attentive Blake would surface. Life would be good, but his hooks and claws were sinking ever deeper into my skin. I felt like he was a parasite steadily sucking me dry.

I should have done more to get rid of him at that stage because my job was intense, and it became a case of fulfillment and respect in my workplace, but the exact opposite at home. Everything I did for Blake was wrong. Apparently, I was stupid and inept. My interests were useless, and I could not have any outside of what Blake wanted.

Our finances were so tight at this point. Blake's spending habits were adding up, and I had credit card debt because of the furnace: something that I had avoided for my entire life until then. I started to press for Blake to look for work, something he had absolutely no drive to do on his own.

Finally, in December, about nine months after we moved cross-country, Blake got a low-paid job as a nursing aid and made me well aware of how miserable he was wiping asses. I had to pay for his uniforms, and it would take him forty-five minutes to get there. Then he had to travel between houses all day. The fuel costs added up. He had to buy himself lunch as well. By the time all was said and done, he was actually losing money.

Meanwhile, I was getting respect at work and enjoying my increasingly less simple tasks. I started to design a large, complex reporting system that was an amazing project to work on; my previous experience performing evaluative services for child welfare organizations made me the leading reporting expert on our team.

To say I was frustrated with Blake was an understatement. He had so much more to offer than being a nursing aid and, because of his experience in the military, he was good at presenting himself, especially in interviews. Why he went for these low-paid jobs was completely beyond me. I was unable to work out the economics of it all. Years later, a few people around town prompted me to wonder if he was going to bars instead of working. I have to wonder if they *knew* he was at the bar on those days or if the job was purposefully bad, so it would be an excuse to stop working entirely. I'm certain it was at least one of those and perhaps both. Maybe he just didn't work as frequently as he claimed.

We also helped an elderly couple clear their driveway of snow that winter; they were too frail to take care of it themselves. The husband died sometime the following year, and the wife was always grateful for what we had done. He might have died much sooner trying to plow that driveway himself. I am glad we did it; Blake had me purchase an expensive new snow-blower anyway, which made it easy.

The flaws in our relationship had developed a bit of consistency at this point. Blake had no sense of the need to budget, no genuine desire to work, was emotionally unstable, and neither of us really enjoyed our physical intimacy. Despite these flaws, I had become emotionally dependent on him and tolerated the warts in our life.

Still, that manipulative narcissist would emerge again from time to time. There were intermittent rounds of berating and gaslighting. It was like Blake had to ensure I knew who was really in control here. If I stepped out of line or tried to have my own life in any way, it was not tolerated and I was punished accordingly. His outbursts felt random, and I had to be careful not to annoy him. Even if I was perpetually walking on eggshells, he would still find something to complain about and couldn't have a reasonable discussion. After some time and repetitiveness on his part, I would join the fray and become inappropriate myself. It turned into long-winded shouting matches that I would eventually give up on and simply resigned myself to being screamed at.

The dichotomy of me gaining respect and power at work while being made to feel stupid and useless at home emerged time and again. Home and work were so different, and I began to normalize insulating one part of life from another. It was emotionally draining and scarring. A general pattern of him blowing up once a month started to develop, but I really didn't notice it. I thought it was instability rather than a conscious decision. I was most likely wrong. The retrospect of patterns emerged while digging through my memories.

Deep down I knew there was something wrong but also knew that the house was too large a task for me to handle on my own. My inability to care for things and fear of responsibility for a home helped keep me trapped by Blake's intermittent madness. Additionally, as soon as the fights were over, he would love-bomb me to get me to forget what had just transpired and bury it behind better memories.

❖ 68 ❖

11. The Cage Rusts

A year and a half after we first met, in January Blake and I attended my grandmother's eightieth birthday party in Atlanta. They had reserved the entire restaurant, so we had it to ourselves. Multiple family members had flown out, many of whom I rarely saw and two of whom were not the most comfortable around gay men. One had minor emotional issues, and the other had more severe ones.

My grandmother, quite the character, had been doing burlesque as a kind of gag. One wife had recently hired her to be a dancer at her husband's birthday party. She had emerged from the cake and made a magnificent spectacle, to everyone's amusement. My grandmother did a bit of her show at her own party by dancing around the room and waving her legs in ways you would not expect an eighty-year-old to be capable of (she could practically do a full split while standing). She is clearly the side of the family I inherited the connective tissue disorder from. They probably didn't have the health issues I had because they had more physically active jobs and were in better shape overall; stronger muscles are one of the primary things you can do to alleviate the issues.

I fondly remembered going to my first pride parade in New York City. The grandmotherly couple and my parents and I had jumped into a random place in the parade and started marching. I was dancing down the street, following a float in front with a mixture of gay and supportive firemen behind. Eventually we got separated from both groups by red lights, and it was just me dancing to my own internal beat through the gayborhood where the parade ended. While on the subway later, my grandmother had swung around a pole said, "I want to be a dancer."

And here again at her birthday party, she was having a great time dancing around and amusing everyone. We were all on our best behavior. Once the pre-dinner fun ended, we were eating our meal and chatting. We had been put at the far end of the table with the other men I mentioned earlier who were closer to our age.

Rather than try to avoid ruining the party and sidestep confrontation, which is what everyone else was doing, Blake most likely became upset that he was not the center of attention and decided to create a problem that would direct attention to him. I don't remember what he said, but he started asking questions and making comments that would clearly upset people who were not comfortable around a gay couple. While the issues were certainly present on their own, the potential troublemakers were perfectly amiable and had been getting along with us just fine. Blake detected that he could create drama, so he baited them into it and one of them, being of lesser self-control than most, took it without thinking. The other came to his cousin's defense.

This almost ruined my grandmother's party because it started an emotional verbal altercation. We mostly managed to keep her separate from it, but it took a lot of work and ruined what would have otherwise been nothing but a good time. With a few others, I spent the evening on crowd control to protect my grandmother from the negativity Blake had raised but was deflecting onto my homophobic cousins. We flew back home in a rather unhappy state.

Eventually, I told Blake to drop the terrible job he had; it was costing more money than he made, and he no longer had time to take care of the house. It left him crabby and unpleasant. We went back to him being a house-husband. He could now do whatever he wanted during the day and went back to being an aggrieved homemaker: perpetually angry at his husband for being controlling and financially abusive by attempting to retain some form of budget and prevent the growing debt spiral.

His spending habits continued regardless. A house always needs some form of investment and housework is difficult without all the latest fancy gadgets. So, debt started to pile up on the credit cards. I kept some pressure on him to find a kind of tolerable employment to relieve my financial burden as well as to give him some kind of place in the world outside of house service.

Blake dropped a huge bombshell in mid-March; about one and a half years after we met. I came home from work to find him hiding in the finished basement. When I came downstairs, without so much as a hello he told me my father had a secret girlfriend and that he sent her sexually explicit love letters via email. I stood there in shock at the bottom of the stairs, my mouth agape.

Blake said my father had somehow cc'd him in by mistake. Without giving me a minute to process this, Blake went into a tirade, demanding that I make my mother aware of exactly what was going on. But how could I? I needed some time to figure out what to do. He said there was no room for discussion and demanded that I notify my mother there and then.

"Blake, give me some time to think about this. I haven't got my head round it all yet and I'm not prepared to blurt out something as serious as this without even having a chance to consider it. Give me a few days to process what I'm learning here. A few hours even. Yes, I agree something needs to happen and it can't be ignored but telling my mother directly is probably not the best way."

'Do you realize how selfish you are? There's your mother, thinking she has a wonderful marriage, and your father is making a complete and utter fool of her. God knows how many other people know and are laughing at her behind her back. You have a duty to her.' Blake was flailing his arms around by this time.

I was thinking that it was unlikely anyone was laughing about this and that it was more likely people felt nothing about guilt if they knew. All I said though was, 'I'm still in shock and just need time to process.'

"NO, YOU NEED TO TELL HER RIGHT NOW!!!!"

I looked at his flushed face as he stomped his right foot on the floor. I had to proceed and deal with him instead of what was really happening. All I wanted was to think, but was not being given the opportunity. Blake's demands just continued, and I eventually blocked them out and retreated to my own headspace so I could think clearly.

Once I ignored his increasingly demeaning words, I was able to process things, and it occurred to me I should make my father tell my mother and give him some time to do so. It took almost twenty minutes of arguing, but Blake finally agreed to give my dad a week.

I called him and had an emotionally painful discussion. He took it well and made it clear he would tell my mother and wanted our relationship to remain undamaged. He was very appreciative that he had time to consider his words and the ability to pick a reasonable time to reveal all. I could hear the emotional anguish in his voice and knew he was upset.

He had been caught and at the time had no idea how he could have cc'd Blake in on this email. My dad had only emailed Blake once before. It had been fairly recent, and Blake seemed to have come up with an excuse for my father to email him in the first place as he otherwise wanted nothing to do with my father.

There were most likely difficult emotional discussions that I will never be privy to, but I was made aware that my mother was willing to forgive my father. He had been unhappy for some time, and so they decided to break up. Looking back, I believe it was for the best, but Blake should never have gotten involved the way he did. He had no right to interfere.

It was perfectly fine to let me know about the love letter, but he should not have demanded my response to it and certainly should have let me think about the situation. It was my family, after all. I know I could never have stood by and let it continue; the point is that it should have been my choice, not his.

Not long after, a breakthrough emerged in Blake's life. The village ambulance service hired him. It was not the best-paying job in the world, but he was good at it and was contributing to the community. It was something for him to take pride in, which was important to us both. On top of that, he loved his chief, who was in a lesbian relationship. It also acted as a small anchor for me in the community, since we were otherwise an island except for the two neighbors we had become friendly with.

There was a minor crisis when his chief and her girlfriend needed a place to stay while they waited for the bank to approve a new home purchase. I was happy to let them stay with us for a month while they completed their home loan. I was slightly less enthused about their seven- and fifteen-year-old daughters, but they would mostly be with their dad.

I really did not want their six dogs: that many animals would ruin stuff, and there was no doubt they would crap all over the carpets. Blake kept at it for weeks to get me to say yes to those dogs. Eventually I gave in. They moved in a week before we left to go to Ohio, and it was not really a problem other than me being annoyed by the presence of the dogs and how freaked out our cats were by their presence.

The trip to Ohio went well. The only noteworthy thing anyone recalls is that Blake spent a lot of time talking about all the nice things I was going to buy for him. When we returned home, we found out that the ladies were unable to leave because their bank was being finicky. This was, to a degree, miserable because the situation had relegated us to the finished basement (where our cats were hiding from the dogs).

We did this to have privacy from the family living upstairs. On the other hand, having witnesses around meant that Blake had to be considerably better behaved. All in all, this was a blessing. Blake had a very firm persona that he wanted to portray to other people. He was false, wearing a mask of lies.

They stayed with us for nearly three months until they finally got their new house, and we got our home back. Blake's behavior mostly modulated heavily in front of other people and the wonderful man he had been for months with our temporary guests around vanished. Like he had been pent up with a need to tear me down.

Overnight, the old Blake resurfaced. He started a five-hour screaming fit the day after they left. It was about literally nothing that was happening. In retrospect, the entire purpose was to tear me down and put me back into my place at his feet. But at the time, I could only argue with his nonsense and feel steadily worse about myself.

After about two hours, I had talked him through various issues, but he immediately went straight back to the beginning and started over as if nothing I said even mattered. I gave up on arguing at this point and waited for it to end. I figured it was one of his emotional fits. He was better the next day, and everything went back to normal again. He simply acted like nothing had occurred.

Later that month was my birthday and Blake utterly destroyed it. When we woke up, I said that I wanted to do something. I don't even remember what, but it was not a big deal. The fact that I might have my own desires on my birthday seriously pissed him off, and so he embarked on an all-day rant, gaslighting, threatening, and berating. Things kicked off minutes after we woke up and did not end until late into the evening. This became a pattern year after year on what should have been a celebration, and I eventually stopped trying to have a birthday; I have not celebrated one since. On the one hand, his birthdays were the complete opposite in that we did whatever he wanted, and I sucked it up even if it wasn't something I was interested in. On the other, that was pretty much the same as every other day when he got what he wanted. So, there wasn't very much difference between his birthday and normal days.

The next day, Blake acted like nothing had happened and asked if I wanted to celebrate my birthday. I decided to break up with him, telling him he was absolutely out of line the day before. This triggered an entire week of fighting. There was no way to get rid of him. Though I had no issues with the local department, the scars of the past remained, and I didn't want to involve the police. I was at my wit's end, sexually frustrated and unfulfilled in every way apart from at work, and Blake denied my needs and derided anything that I took an interest in. We spent our time together smoking weed and watching TV.

I desperately needed to get rid of him and had to find a way. Every time we were at home, the discussions were like legal inquisitions. We never had a rational discussion about why we were together or how we could separate. I tried everything to convince Blake that he had his own life to live and had to transition so that he was not so dependent on me. As always, he agreed to concessions. He said he would change his behavior, but the truth was he never stuck to anything.

One thing scared me quite a lot. I had taken out life insurance through work, and Blake was the recipient. The crux of the matter was that if I died, a fairly large amount of money would go to Blake, which is normal in any relationship with a financial arrangement. Around the time I set it up, Blake started making jokes about killing me off for profit. Deep down, I knew it was the beginning of the end, but I suppressed it and played it down as best I could.

We had not had sex for months and I was frustrated and confused without any outlet for my pain. Late at night, I crept downstairs to the basement and started secretly having cyber-sex with other men via chat rooms (online writing only descriptive fantasies). It really turned me on and acted as an emotional release. I enjoyed increasingly violent fantasies via chat and eventually transitioned into the victim rather than the perpetrator.

Some of the men wanted to meet me and initially, I arranged a few meetings but always backed out because I considered it a betrayal towards Blake. I was cautious about logging out of my Yahoo account and am certain I did so the day in question, but when I came home from work Blake revealed that he had accessed my Yahoo email account and found out what I was doing. He said he just went to the Yahoo mail site and it was already logged in.

We got into a huge fight, and he accused me of meeting the men. I denied it, but he never believed me. Unfortunately, there was one email where I had agreed to meet up but ultimately flaked on the meeting without further contact between the two of us.

Blake blackmailed me. He said if I ever kicked him out, he would tell everyone that I had cheated on him. The story he described did not even match what was in the emails, but the truth existed only to be twisted around and act as a slight anchor to the reality he wanted to be portrayed. This was when Blake took any remaining subtlety away from his abuse. It became the perfect excuse for him to exercise complete control. Anytime we disagreed this would emerge as a cudgel and threat. He seemed quite ecstatic about having this new tool.

I soon learned that he had performed interrogations in Afghanistan during the Cheney years. Apparently, I was attached to someone I had read about in a news article years before we met; he would play detainees the "Barney" theme song continuously until they broke. It took about eighteen hours of this before they cracked and gave up all the information the military wanted from them.

Blake also informed me that his fellow interrogators from Afghanistan were still at high levels of the U.S. government, including the NSA, an agency that has access to all our communications. These folks were still not too keen on following all the rules. What's the point of being able to view everyone's communications if you can't even bully your girlfriends? They didn't mind that it was a male this time. I'm not sure how much of this I believed, but given how many times I nearly died later, I would be shocked if it wasn't true.

Blake told me that his buddies had noticed my father communicating with his girlfriend last spring via email because they were overseas at the time. This enabled them to spy on the communications because the rules let them look at anything that crossed the national border. They had plotted together how to make it seem like Blake had learned by accident. I have no idea if it was true.

Blake continued threatening to tell everyone I had cheated on him—if I didn't give him things he wanted. And he used this threat as a constant cudgel to make me feel lower than dirt. Blake was now in total control and knew it. Life at home became more about being abused than anything else.

12. Cost of Separation

Emotional abuse was regular and expected. I tried to discuss separation, but it was not a topic to be broached without days of punishment for even considering it. I would go to work and live out a happy, normal day. A steady stream of people started to appear at my door wanting advice about how to proceed with their work; I even recall a line forming outside my office at some point. I would come back from a break and sit down to write out pages of code that just ran the first time they were executed and was effectively managing the patient-portal analytics team as well as part of a related company-wide oversight council.

At home, there was a new horror show on a regular basis. I crept around the house doing anything to keep the peace, but it ultimately made no difference.

By spring, about six months after my parents' divorce, Blake had been going out drinking during the week for quite a while and was spending mostly my money to do it. Somehow, his extra earnings never made it into the household budget. Everything from there was a downhill slide into misery, and I was just a mark to be controlled and used. The abuse sessions were no longer subtle, they were targeted to ensure I kept my place gloomily at his feet.

Our relationship was all about me providing him with the money he wanted. At some point, I really should have gone to the police, but he would have simply flipped the switch and acted like he had no idea what I was talking about.

After one of these outings, Blake came home extremely drunk with clear physical indications that he had bottomed. He strenuously denied it, but there were no other explanations, and it was obvious. He had also started spending prolifically with my credit card on purpose.

I was racking up serious debt. Life was hopeless at this point, as he felt he had enough hooks in me, believing that there was no way I could ever walk away from the relationship. He had no qualms about spending as much time employing any tactic necessary to quell attempts to separate. How else could he support himself? Besides, abusing me was fun.

At some point that summer, a breakthrough in Blake's life occurred. He met a college professor who had agreed to take him under his wing and worked hard to get him accepted on a full scholarship. Blake wanted to experience campus life and live there. Suddenly, he was interested in leaving the boring house so he could hang out in dorms and hook up with young college guys from a more sexually fluid generation.

It became less difficult to discuss the problems of our relationship and Blake agreed to leave because it was what he wanted—but not without exacting a price. He had maxed out three of my credit cards shortly before he left and had a host of demands—or else he would tell everyone I cheated on him. He moved out to live in a dorm apartment near the gay bars downtown shortly before the school year started. I paid for everything and was happy to get rid of him.

But now, apart from the two cats, I was alone in an enormous house that I was unable to afford and had not even wanted in the first place. Meanwhile, the surrounding community was from a culture very different from my own and practically an hour from anything I would typically want to do. My debt was unmanageable. It was impossible to make my monthly payments on the house, and I missed at least one credit card payment. What a transformation! When we met, there was a small but tidy sum in my accounts, with no debt whatsoever.

Then the interest rate on my cards skyrocketed to 25 percent, and there was nothing I could do about it. I didn't even have the energy to look after the property properly. Blake had wiped me out completely, mentally, physically, and financially.

I knew that if I sold the house, I would probably lose money I didn't have, so I had no actual option but to stick it out. Like a pauper, I lived from day to day in order to cover the monthly expenses. I tried to find a roommate, but everybody wanted to be in the city. I should probably have declared bankruptcy, but it felt morally unacceptable to walk away, and it might have impeded my ability to get a white-collar job in the future.

I eventually realized that Blake had socially isolated me during our time together and that he had cut me off from most of the people I had previously known. I became depressed, but my work was an absolute godsend to me. Then, I was designing the replacement framework for the system I had worked on primarily. I was becoming the team software architect, albeit not being paid much to do so. It was the only part of my day I could stand, and the money for lunch and breakfast came out of future paychecks; so I could eat. Dinner ended up going away so I could pay the bills.

Each evening as I returned home, it was as if a black cloud drifted over me. The cats stopped getting along and started fighting. Mickey eventually cuddled with me for the first time since I had met him two years before. This made my cat jealous; she would slap Mickey and then, when he got angry, run into the room like he was bullying her to get him in trouble. Not a pleasant situation with animals, especially without Blake around to enforce the peace. I eventually relented to the spray bottle, but derived no joy from it the way Blake did. It fortunately did not take too many sprays to reduce the frequency of the fights.

I did have some evening reprieves with the newly retired neighbor Nancy. We drank wine and chatted in the evening hours from time to time. I also spent a lot of time online. Mostly having what were increasingly dark sexual fantasies, living out the reality I had been in, but at a more explicit and entirely sexual level.

I eventually met a few people and invited them over. One in particular had brought some GHB with him: a drug generally used as a date rape drug. He talked me into taking a half dose with him recreationally. I figured it would be a good idea, so I recognized the feeling and was perhaps less prone to the effects. What a misery that was. I spent the next two hours on the toilet.

Fortunately, the guy had thought it would be enjoyable for us (I guess it was for him) and was not trying to do anything untoward. He stayed there with me, helping me through it, and we ultimately enjoyed our time together. I even went up to visit him where he lived on the other side of the state.

Back home, I could see no way out of my debt and had little hope of selling the house to cover what I owed, but I had gotten to the point where I could at least live frugally but comfortably. Except for the loneliness.

Blake had left his car in the driveway. He had stopped making monthly payments on it. At some point my battery died, and I tried to jumpstart my car using his. I cross-wired it and completely destroyed his car, which would no longer start. Mine, on the other hand, continued to function but acted funny from time to time. Eventually, the repo company came for Blake's car, so it was not my problem.

About three months after we separated, something amazing was happening nationally and gay marriage was becoming legal. The nearby state of Illinois soon started to officially allow it. On top of that, the "Don't Ask Don't Tell" policy was repealed. Gays were now welcome in the military.

In retrospect, it was most likely not a coincidence that Blake contacted me again around this time. Everything that happened next was a conscious, well-thought-out, and nefarious plan.

13. A Devious New Plan

Those first few phone calls were very strained. I wanted nothing to do with him. I did congratulate him upon learning that his discharge from the army had been upgraded from general to honorable because of the repeal of "Don't Ask, Don't Tell"; this meant that he could now receive a slew of army related benefits. It also potentially opened the path to him rejoining, which he was considering. His classes were going well, and he seemed to have his life in order.

He was full of energy, and I was so drained and in need. He knew how to bring me joy, dig me out of the emotional hole I was in, and make me feel alive again. He was a rollercoaster ride of powerful emotions in an otherwise bleak and empty sea of melancholy.

Blake invited me out a few times to the bar and provided a place to crash locally. He brought the fun back into my life. We ended up doing more than just sleeping next to each other a few times. He eventually decided to help clean up the financial mess he left me in and mentioned that his army benefits now included a debt consolidation service that was available to anyone he was in a relationship with. The service wasn't too particular about officialdom, so we both agreed we were in a relationship again. But not exclusively or with the intent of being fully back together as Blake was enjoying the student population, and I was still wary of him.

The debt consolidation went through, and I suddenly had a manageable payment that would eventually go away. My life improved significantly because I had money to go out and enjoy life again. I was spending more time with Blake, and he was being his best instead of his worst. At this stage, he was back to pumping me up for harvest later. He ultimately rejoined the army via the reserves. He seemed to have his act together and was working on the paperwork.

It suddenly got cold, very cold; they called it the Polar Vortex. It's a weather pattern change that causes arctic weather to reach its withering hand down the entire upper Midwest. Temperatures dropped from −20° to −50°F for three months straight. My car acted up and wouldn't start on the coldest days. This was most likely caused by my poor attempt at jump starting it; every component had become slightly delicate.

I came up with a plan to get to work reliably by living with Blake in his one-room apartment so I could take the bus in from there (the small town my house was in didn't offer a reasonable bus service). It was a two-block walk in the frigid cold; fortunately, I had a crazy thick feather jacket and a scarf to cover my mouth so the air wouldn't freeze my lungs and nostrils. Breathing was still painful though. There was an app that gave me a five-minute warning of the bus arrival time, so the wait outside wasn't long.

I received several texts from my family while working. My grandmother had COPD; a smoking-related illness that makes it almost impossible to breathe. She was hospitalized and most likely dying. I informed work and flew out to Atlanta alone on a last-minute flight. On my arrival, I saw she was unconscious on a continuous morphine drip in a hospital bed. I was told she was unlikely to regain consciousness and that my last opportunity to speak to her was gone.

There we were, my family and my grandmother's friends all together in a full room. Suddenly, my grandmother rose from her completely immobile state and gave me an enormous hug, clasping me with great strength. She wasn't really awake and couldn't speak, so I did. "Everyone who loves you is here. We were told you were unlikely to recover. It's okay, Grandma. We all love you and know that you love us. We'll miss you, but don't want you to suffer. You can let go if it's the right thing to do." That hug was her last action in life, and I'll never forget the love I felt coming from her at that moment.

I flew back to Madison and returned to Blake, who was in a wooing phase with me. Blake inquired about inheritance, and I wasn't immediately certain how that would pan out but knew Grandma wasn't particularly wealthy. He suggested that annuities could be quite large, but I was dismissive of the possibility. Blake and I soon started to act more like a couple. He knew I wanted out of the house we had owned together, and he helped kick a process into gear to get it sold. It took a while to get things in order and no buyers immediately surfaced.

After about a month, I learned that Grandma had left her shared home to her partner. Among those I was close to, no one begrudged this, but in retrospect Blake looked annoyed about it. I was then told there was ten years of annuity payments coming at $450 a month. It was another several weeks later that I found out the payment was being split among multiple people, so it didn't amount to much. I thought the miscommunication was funny, but Blake was quite disappointed.

I eventually found a buyer at a loss. The new owner was even excited about the organ in the basement, a permanent, unremovable fixture at this point. I was relieved to be done with it all. The beautiful, perennial, dinner plate-sized bright red hibiscus flowers we had planted didn't survive that insanely cold winter. It was quite a coincidence.

At some point during that spring, Blake was accepted into the army reserves. He would give them one weekend a month, and they became part of his life again. He had rescued me from the mess he'd created, promised forgiveness for my mistakes, and had a full life plan. Things were looking good, and I ultimately agreed to be in a full relationship with him again.

With the house gone, my finances were mostly corrected. And so, after living full time in a one room college dorm, we decided to move into a small one-bedroom apartment. It was in a great location for both of us. Interestingly enough, Blake was quite insistent that I sleep on the opposite side of the bed than I had always slept on before. He wanted me on the inside, away from the door. In retrospect, every time we had ever slept together, he was holding the exit. I wasn't aware of the reasoning at first.

This was when Blake started talking about getting married. He discussed me receiving army benefits, but I didn't need them. He made it clear the culture of the armed services insisted on a full marriage; otherwise, it wouldn't give me any credence. I told him marriage was not on the cards at the moment. I was okay being together casually, without commitments, but not comfortable enough to tie the knot. Somewhere deep down, I must have sensed Blake was luring me into a trap. These thoughts stayed in my subconscious, and

I recall the feeling of apprehension anytime he brought up marriage. He kept at it though and was persistent for weeks, but I held my ground. Suddenly, he seemed to give up. He couldn't let it go completely, though. He had his plan and was going to see it through. So, he eventually utilized a tactic generally reserved for prisoners of war.

One Monday evening, I came home from work and Blake wanted a drink at our usual bar, the respectable neighborhood gay bar. I reminded him it was a work night, but hesitantly agreed to go along because he was adamant. We had a good night but unfortunately, the night lasted longer than I had anticipated, and we got home at two o'clock in the morning.

The following day was a tough day at work, and I was absolutely exhausted when I returned home.

"I need something light to eat and I want an early night in bed," I told him as I collapsed onto the sofa.

Blake had other ideas and wouldn't take no for an answer. He wanted to go out again, so he pleaded with me for a good thirty minutes and wouldn't let it go. He refused to go out alone. I eventually gave in and agreed. There was a pattern developing here, but I didn't have any idea it was a malicious plan.

We stayed out until two in the morning again, and I went to work even more exhausted than the previous day. I managed to get through my work and came home, collapsing on the sofa again.

"We're going out," Blake announced.

"No way," I replied.

But he went on and on until eventually I broke down again. He was right back to his old self, but somehow, I didn't recognize he had crushed my spirit. My brain wasn't working properly due to lack of sleep. All this came out of the blue after months of him being a reasonable, sweet, caring man.

The third night out also went until two o'clock. I got a half night's sleep for the third day in a row before going back to work. I remember waking up and downing several glasses of water before my thirty-minute commute. When I got there, I still wasn't awake and had to pee so badly it hurt.

I wandered directly into the bathroom, which had a single urinal. I used to joke with a coworker that the way they were designed I might one day wander up and start peeing without noticing someone was already standing there. This was the only day where that almost happened. I was so dazed that I had already unzipped before noticing someone else was already there. I took a surprised lurch backwards then stood there slack-jawed, half awake, and desperately waiting for him to finish while dancing slightly.

After perhaps twenty seconds of waiting, I realized the stall was open and rushed in, making a loud, relieved sound as I finally let it all go. The man later accused me of watching him urinate, but indicated I might have been hungover and not awake yet. It was clearly the latter, but by the time the accusation had surfaced, I didn't even remember this event.

I was almost dead when I arrived home that evening. This was when Blake really laced into me about getting married. It was five hours of what, in retrospect, was an interrogation session. He had implemented a classic military maneuver, three days of sleep deprivation to wear down the mind of his target, then emotional abuse to get his way. He kept escalating until I simply couldn't say no anymore. I was too tired to make coherent arguments, too out of whack to resist. Blake was a professional at this after all. Remember that he told me that this was one of his functions in Afghanistan during the Cheney years? It isn't too surprising he was successful.

I'm not sure why I didn't back out in the first few weeks, but Blake switched to his better self and coaxed things along. These were some of our happiest times together. Due to our marriage agreement, we were effectively engaged. The army was trying to integrate gays and had an opportunity to do so. They invited me to attend a formal military ball. I suspect they would normally have waited until after marriage, but a gay couple was probably beneficial to the culture to reinforce the new norm.

I was excited by the prospect. Perhaps there was some trepidation that something could go horribly wrong, but I mostly wanted to make sure that if it did, it wasn't my fault. There was a pretty good chance there would be at least one person with a problem. It didn't matter to me because it was nice to ride at the forefront of a cultural shift; some risk comes with the territory.

The commanding officer and his wife greeted us straight away. I was being treated as a VIP. They needed the evening to go down well because it would obviously be a potential media quagmire if it didn't. The wives were elated to have a unique personality in their social mix. I got the feeling they lived insulated lives on the military bases and were kind of bored because they interacted primarily with other military housewives who shared similar circumstances. A gay man thrown into the mix would seriously spice things up (socially), and they were excited by the prospect of someone new and interesting.

I remember being cautious about going to the bathroom; it was unnecessary. We were outside smoking cigarettes when some guy made a slightly offhand comment that I don't even recall. It was not the most offensive thing someone could say, but it wasn't particularly appropriate. He was immediately grabbed and discharged by the next day. In my mind, I wondered if it had been an overreaction, but Blake was quite pleased with the outcome. I felt bad that someone's career was over for what seemed like a trivial comment that was more tactless than hurtful. I also remember being hit on by one guy. He was testing the waters inquiring about a threesome with me as their bottom: a position I'd had here and there but hadn't frequented. I have to admit I was intrigued but not immensely interested in bottoming, as I find it painful. Still, it was exciting to be a fringe member of army life. I didn't mind having to face a few headwinds, and the vast majority of the people really didn't seem to mind at all or at least kept their reservations to themselves if they did.

Blake and I planned out two separate weddings. For some reason, he wanted to have a religious ceremony, which was totally strange to me since I'd rarely attended any form of sacred service and was principally raised as an agnostic.

Blake's only connection to church was when he worked as an organist and he never espoused any affinity for religion either. He wanted to use a synagogue to recognize my half-Jewish heritage. This enabled us to have a local service on top of the municipal one in Chicago.

I suspect the religious ceremony would have been more meaningful to Blake's mother, and he wanted her to attend. She insisted I pay for her travel from upstate New York, but I didn't feel that I should be obligated to cover her travel costs. Generally, the host pays for the actual parties and services. I probably should have relented and paid since it would have meant so much to Blake, but I stood firm and he didn't go into paratrooper mode to press the issue. I suspect he was too nervous about potentially upsetting the actual marriage plan.

We had the legal ceremony, which entailed receiving a certificate in a government office building. There was also a very nice dinner, which my father and my grandmother's surviving partner attended. I had the feeling Blake was trying to segregate my father from the larger affair, as he wasn't particularly fond of him. My parents were on speaking terms, having had a much healthier separation than Blake and me. But my mother was not fond of the idea of spending time with her ex-husband. She did not mention this to me, it just went without saying.

A sizable gathering of my friends flew in to attend the religious ceremony. People from college, relatives who rarely traveled, my mother, and some coworkers. Blake had a few local friends as well, but his side of the family was noticeably absent. It might explain why my parents described me as looking overjoyed and him as appearing somber; like he was doing an onerous duty. This was another sign I should have noticed about Blake; the people in his past weren't interested in his future.

Things were amazing between Blake and me for a while, but one thing was a complete U-turn from how our life had been pre-wedding. Blake stopped wanting to be intimate immediately after the marriage. When we did have sex, it felt more like he was doing his wifely duty than wanting to participate. The shift was overnight. He otherwise stayed his better self, but started gently prodding me for a few things.

The first was that he wanted me to sign up for a master's level course in computer science. They were offering them on campus at work. I didn't really need a class for anything. Working in the field for many years with a bachelor's degree in computer science is generally sufficient. Blake was unrelenting. Plus, when I inquired further, it looked like an interesting class, so I asked my manager if the company would pay for the course. He agreed, though he was slightly confused because I didn't need it for anything. It was taught one night a week and would keep me at work until nine in the evening. I'd also be involved with homework.

I eventually figured out the purpose of the class was to keep me busy; this was just a backup plan though. Blake also prodded me to change the benefactor of my various life insurance plans at work.

By the time those changes went through, it was four years after I had initially met Blake and less than a month after we got married. My birthday was about three weeks away and the paperwork to switch my life insurance plans for setting Blake as the benefactor had gone through. It was time to execute.

14. Pulling the Trigger

Blake again became insistent we go out on a weeknight, and so we found ourselves drinking in the gayborhood bar. One of our drinking partners was Blake's friend Michelle, the daughter of a famous coach. She lived two blocks from the bar.

Michelle was another awesome character. She had a law license, despite having multiple disabilities: these included cerebral palsy, autism, a childlike demeanor and confidence issues. Strangely enough, she had a crush on Blake, despite being fully aware that he was gay and married. She was likeable and easy to get along with; I did not feel threatened by or jealous of her crush at all. Hindsight is a wonderful thing. But, again, I now know Blake saw her as an asset and nothing more.

We proceeded to get incredibly drunk, and I was aware at one point Michelle wanted to go home. Blake insisted that we go to a different bar for one more drink and that we would drive because it was closer to our apartment. After the drive—and literally one quick drink—she had no way home, so she had to crash on our couch. Blake was insistent about it, and nobody really resisted. He needed a pliable witness, and I didn't mind her presence.

When I got to bed, I remember the room was spinning, and all I wanted to do was close my eyes and go to sleep. I collapsed onto the bed. Blake walked into the room and announced that he wanted sex. I couldn't believe it. Not satisfied with intimacy on a quiet night when we were at home alone, he wanted it now when I was barely coherent. I had no interest in sex whatsoever, especially since Michelle was in the other room.

Too drunk to even take my clothes off, I closed my eyes. Blake was getting angry and insisted that I go get some water.

I was nearly asleep. "Why can't you get it?" I asked.

But of course, Blake was not interested in being reasonable. Instead, he pestered me to serve water for us to drink in the middle of the night; he went on and on. I was barely sober enough to stand, but he badgered me until I finally got up and fetched two enormous glasses of water.

What happened next was so bizarre. As I closed my eyes once again, I could hear more demands for sex, but I ignored them. And as I was about to drift into a hypnotic state, he dumped an entire glass of water on me, soaking the bed.

My eyes sprung open, and I lay there, deciding how to react. My dormant terror of his rage fits was now wide awake. I knew if I made any missteps, we'd be arguing until morning and that I wouldn't get any sleep. I needed to get to work the next day. If I screamed at him for soaking the bed, I knew I would lose any ensuing arguments and be painted as a monster. I mostly just wanted peace. So, to avoid confrontation, I decided to be playful.

I grabbed my glass and attempted to throw the water in his face. Unfortunately, both my hands and the glass were wet, and the glass slipped out of my hand. I hadn't meant to hit him, but the glass bounced off his temple. It probably hurt. Then it smashed into what seemed like hundreds of little pieces in the corner. He screamed at me as I stared at him in doe-eyed fear. He rushed over to me, but I passed out on the bed.

The next thing I remember is waking up in a standing position. My body was trying to retreat, and I had bumped up against the window. Something was slapping me in the eyes repeatedly. Not so it hurt, but so I couldn't open them and kept getting a jarring light slap to my eyelids.

I had no idea what was going on and didn't remember where I was or how I got there. I eventually figured out it was a person slapping me and gave them a light shove in the center of their chest to create some space.

I opened my eyes to figure out what was happening. What I witnessed might have been worthy of an Oscar. Waiting a split second too long, Blake took three or four intentionally enormous steps backward. He staggered towards the nightstand. And then, he made a production of his knees buckling; he fell, and at the same time, threw his head towards the corner of the small end table by the door. It seemed purposeful, like he aimed for it, but I wasn't sure.

Blake had a small, bloodied wound on his temple. I became concerned about his welfare, got up, and walked over to him. He was standing in the doorway blocking the exit and I was about six feet from him.

"We have to get you to a hospital," I said.

But Blake didn't care about that at all.

"You attacked me and now I have the right to defend myself!" Blake shrieked.

"I never attacked you!" I protested.

He yelled in an accusatory tone, "You just shoved me into this dresser!"

"No, I had no idea what was going on. You were slapping my eyes. I couldn't see anything, and I think I blacked out. I pushed whatever was hitting me away and didn't even push that hard. You stumbled across the entire room. You didn't go flying into it," I explained.

I wondered quietly if he had decisively hit his head against the dresser. His steps backward had been so exaggerated and he turned towards the nightstand before aiming at it.

"Fine, you attacked me with a glass!" Blake yelled.

"No, I didn't. You threw water at me and I was going to do the same to you. My hands were wet and I'm drunk. I didn't mean for the glass to slip. I'm sure it hurt but you didn't have any injuries from that and I passed out right after! I'm sorry you are hurt now, but we should get you to a hospital," I went on.

"It doesn't matter. I get to take you out and say I had to defend myself from you now," Blake blurted out as an evil grin spread across his face.

This was when I realized why he'd consistently been standing in front of the door, so I couldn't escape. I still had to try to bolt for it so I could hopefully get by him. He quite skillfully grabbed me as I tried to pass and pushed me onto the bed on my back, leaping onto my chest. He put his hands around my neck and started to choke me. Although he had fifty pounds on me, I had been trained in this exact situation and humped my hips in an upward direction, attempting to wriggle onto my side and slide out from underneath him.

But I was drunk and obviously, because the bed was soft, I sank into it and couldn't pull it off. He was heavy. Slowly but surely, I felt the oxygen leaving my body, and I knew that if I passed out, I was in deep trouble. I tried twice more and failed both times. I was not going to last much longer and knew death was imminent. Leaving my physical body, I went entirely into the landscape of my mind, searching for a solution. I suddenly bolted back to alertness. Something inside me provided a solution, gravity, and leverage.

I could feel that my left knee was on the inside of his right knee, just a couple of inches from the side of the bed. I simply swiped my leg left and had better leverage from this angle. It was easy to push his knee off the side of the bed. Gravity now became my friend instead of my enemy as I swung both legs off the bed and used my feet to help land him to the floor. My combat instincts told me to incapacitate him, and I could have easily done this by kicking him hard in the knee and dislocating it. I really didn't want to do that to my spouse, so I didn't and bolted for the open door.

As I reached the exit, he was on me again and pulled me back into the room. I stood there in terror when he told me he couldn't let me leave because I was a danger to the world. I couldn't risk him getting on top of me again because he was stronger than me. He had almost killed me, after openly declaring his intention to do so. Afraid for my life, I realized I had no choice but to hit him. I decided on a punch below the nose but didn't hit him with much power, avoiding all the force multipliers I know. I didn't even draw blood, but it worked, and he staggered back in a state of shock. He immediately came to his senses and wanted to go to bed.

His plan had failed. I wasn't going to let him kill me, so it was time to enact his backup plan. As for me, I needed to leave and get help, take him to a hospital, but he continued to block that door. I was so exhausted and bed was all I wanted. Peace at any price, so I agreed to just go to bed with him.

15. Covering His Tracks

In the morning, Blake got up at the same time as me and made a beeline for Michelle, who had been on the couch and had heard the entire affair. I went to the bathroom and got ready to leave the apartment while he was busy in the living room. He stopped me before I could leave. He needed to establish his truth about the events of the previous night with me as well.

While Blake and I were arguing about what happened, Michelle initially supported my view of events, but Blake pressed her and used his usual manipulation tactics to override her viewpoint and get her to believe his story. Now I know why he had brought her home that evening. It was all part of his plan. She rapidly relented, not wanting to be argumentative. Her childlike demeanor made her a pliable witness; it was easy for Blake to muddy the waters.

I wasn't allowed to leave without agreeing to his story; that I had attacked him in a fit of rage. He was also insistent on me wearing a turtleneck and keeping it up all day. I did not know why but eventually succumbed to all his conditions and left for work.

I did not want to linger in the car, fearful he would know if anything unexpected happened, so I turned the engine on, looked around, and started driving. I do not know why I didn't stop once I was on my way, but I couldn't face the truth and perhaps was now in my automatic daily drive routine. It was too terrible, the whole experience cut too deep and so I denied the reality of what had taken place and went about my day. After turning down the neck of my sweater, my coworkers noticed the red marks. I denied it even to them when they asked. I refused help when I needed it most.

After getting home, Blake blackmailed me and said he'd tell everyone I attacked him in a fit of rage if we broke up or if I spoke of what happened. This was Blake's backup plan to alienate me from large swaths of the community by claiming I abused him.

It was Joseph Goebbels, the Nazi Minister of Propaganda, who once said, "If you tell a big enough lie and tell it frequently enough, it will be believed." A tactic you see in modern-day politics.

I could relate to that. Blake was a first-class expert in manipulating perceptions through the use of repetitive falsehoods. Never let your victim have time to think. Keep the moment going by rapidly jumping from one thing to the next. Allow no chance for air, no chance to stop and think, or your victim might clear their head enough to make better decisions. The scope of my work, practically managing the team at this point by being the primary architect (without the title or salary) and providing internal support while also doing development, all helped to keep my mind fully engaged.

By this stage of the game, Blake had given up on killing me and needed to keep me intimidated in order to retain control. He was blaming my punch for affecting his teeth while also undermining my confidence in myself through gaslighting. As long as I quietly went along with things, he would do nothing more than remind me that the fight was all my fault.

Blake spent the next three weeks pulling and pushing at a tooth he said was annoying him and blamed the punch. It may or may not have been complete nonsense. I hadn't hit him very hard, but the location was a potentially delicate one for the tooth in question. The thing is, there is never any reason to push and pull hard on your teeth repeatedly, and he was doing this all the time. I kept telling him not to.

His claim that the root canal he had in the fields of Afghanistan was suddenly painful was likely fallacious. He had actually complained about that particular tooth for years. I later found he had never been to the dentist once during our entire relationship. I probably should have known that if I wasn't paying, it wasn't happening. But it had never been mentioned, and it never occurred to me that I should ask. After all, Blake had so much free time during the day; I had just assumed he was caring for himself.

I was beginning to doubt myself because the more time Blake had to reinforce his story, the more I forgot about what actually happened and believed his version of events. I knew I had been extremely drunk and had forgotten a lot of what had happened on that night.

It was so traumatic my mind couldn't fathom it and much of the evening would remain shrouded in clouds. Blake reinforced his version of events by degrading me and applying his enhanced interrogation techniques to wear me down emotionally. He now had complete control.

Suddenly, on the day before my birthday, that tooth came out. We managed to get an emergency medical appointment to seal the wound. Blake now had his story: I had punched his teeth out in a fit of rage.

The timing gave him another opportunity to ruin my birthday, which was clouded by the emergency surgery the day prior. I wasn't even planning to mention that it was my birthday, but Blake did and snidely asked if we would do anything while displaying his now missing tooth. I quietly shook my head no.

I became even busier as the college course began. Meanwhile, our relationship seemed to improve. Blake started being reasonable again. He had me by the balls and was in control. As long as I went along, things were joyful and smooth. I had a small bit of room to breathe, just enough to get by.

He next insisted that as a married couple, we needed to own a home, but I told him that my finances hadn't fully recovered, and we wouldn't be able to afford one. It was a blessing that he was in the reserves and would get a paycheck from time to time, so perhaps it could be done.

Blake did some research and found a very nice condo on the eastside of town. It was reasonably priced, one that we could easily afford, well within my budget. It was actually a pretty good deal, and I liked the space it offered. Eventually, a guest pointed out some char marks around windows across the street. They were from a meth lab explosion a few years prior. For those who don't know, meth is among the worst of drugs: right up there with injectables like heroin. This explained the low property prices.

The only issue I knew about then was that the condo was forty-five minutes from work and that my commute was now outside the acceptable range for me. It would make my days longer, and in a medium-sized community like ours, it shouldn't have been necessary. If we were in a large city, it would have made more sense. It hadn't occurred to me at the time, but Blake's car had been repossessed, so he would want mine. This location also required a bus transfer, which meant a one-and-a-half-hour commute for me anytime he needed my car. This was a significant feature for Blake because it gave him total freedom during the day without needing to worry about me popping home unexpectedly.

I ultimately agreed to the purchase because I liked the condo. It was actually a space I didn't mind owning; it was the location that wasn't ideal. Once we moved in, Blake regularly needed my car, and I ended up on that long bus route. As well as the commute, my evening class ended at 9 p.m. on Tuesdays, after the bus stopped running. This meant Blake would pick me up at work. This kept me away for even longer periods of time while classwork kept me busy at home.

We started drinking regularly and went through two bottles of wine a night and were smoking a lot of weed. Blake had to drink a chemical cover to avoid the army drug tests. He had to drink the stuff two hours before his test and chug a bunch of water. One week, he specifically mentioned to me that they always test after an accident. The next week, a water buffalo (a huge and heavy water tank) fell on his foot. I was contacted and asked to go to his base so he could be collected and taken to the hospital. I was aghast and rushed there. We went together and sat for about two hours before he had his foot X-rayed and splinted. I was then to take him back to base, where he was immediately drug tested and his contract was summarily terminated after they detected marijuana.

On reflection, I strongly suspect that Blake's job had lost its usefulness, which was a wedge for the marriage and to dupe me into thinking he'd cleaned up his act. The regimented structure of the army was not for Blake; jobs were boring, and army personnel were difficult to deal with at best. Blake was still busy with school though, and it became his daytime focus.

The evenings were about fancy dinners, wine, weed, and partying. My desires were unimportant. If I decided to stay home, it was then a good thing because Blake could go out and do whatever he pleased and pay with my credit card.

The situation soon got even harder to deal with than when we lived in the small town. Blake knew his version of events had solidified and that I was fully cudgeled into the corner. If I stepped out of line, or made any kind of mistake, he would shift into a huge, degrading tantrum that sucked all the oxygen out of the room and beat me down into a helpless emotional wreck. Sometimes the mistakes were made up, other times they might have warranted a quick request for improvement or a minor annoyed outburst. This kept me tiptoeing on eggshells, terrified of displeasing him. Meanwhile, if I had any legitimate complaints, an even more intense round of berating quickly drowned them out. Blake could do no wrong.

I had become a shadow of my former self, always afraid of what was going to happen next. It was kind of ironic. One of my friends had commissioned an art piece for our wedding. It was a painting of Blake and me. For some reason, the artist had chosen to portray Blake as a powerful military figure, with me being slightly blurred out in the background. This was a telling prophecy of how I felt during our marriage. I just went along on a leash, permanently tense and afraid.

I didn't know anything about what was actually happening at Blake's college, but from his telling, it was going well. He was going to graduate at the end of the following semester, giving him a leg up into the next level of society.

On one occasion, we hosted a sizable dinner party for Blake's friends around town. He needed the car, so I had to take the bus to work and he wanted me home promptly at six o'clock the evening of the event. This was almost impossible due to the ten-minute walk when I transferred and the three-minute window between buses. I generally waited around for the next transfer, but this time I tried to make it by running and barely caught the bus. Breathless, I rushed in at exactly six o'clock to find an enormous group of people in my condo.

Blake immediately started barking at me from the kitchen and I rushed in to help.

"Make yourself useful and cut up these vegetables. Do it as quickly as you can."

"But the guests are here already. Why haven't you started yet?"

"Just get it done, NOW!"

Shaking, I took the knife from him but didn't know where to start. I was so stressed out from my workday and trying to catch that bus, I ended up giving myself a nasty gash that bled profusely. I threw the knife onto the counter and set off to bandage the wound myself, although, if I remember right, someone may have helped. It wasn't Blake.

One guest took over chopping the vegetables. I probably should have gone to hospital; instead, I sat dizzy and in pain. I think I may have even helped cook later in the evening but pretended nothing was wrong.

Another guest voiced his thoughts. Why was so little care given to me? But his concerns largely went unnoticed. I sat silently in a daze of pain.

The guests grew frustrated because dinner was almost ready but wasn't served until nine o'clock, a time when most people can't eat an enormous meal. Everyone was resigned to sticking around, as they loved his meal but were obviously irritated at the late hour. This was, of course, very typical of Blake and his presentation of meals.

We continued to pretend we had a fortunate marriage. I was busy with homework and school finishing late while Blake spent hours at the bar and on his degree. We were almost never sober together. Blake was regularly cooking large, fancy meals for us. We would act romantic and in love over delicious dinners. My memories of being strangled truly faded. I got caught back up in the act. Blake, however, couldn't let too much time pass without another horror to keep me in line.

16. Thanksgiving Horror

Thanksgiving rolled around and we planned to visit Blake's family in upstate New York, which was an eighteen-hour drive. Blake convinced Michelle to come along, and we were picking my mother up in Ohio along the way. Not long before we left, I found out that my mother had been in a car accident while she was visiting her family in Ohio and was going to be wheelchair-bound for the trip. She arranged to have a portable chair and for us to pick her up in Ohio instead of N.Y. We barely had enough room in the car for everyone's things, never mind extra equipment. We had to stop at my mother's home in southern upstate N.Y. to get some of the winter gear she was going to need for an extended trip to Ohio. She couldn't take care of herself in her two-story home as a wheelchair user and had no other way to travel than in our car.

Michelle was having anxiety attacks due to the overcrowding of the car, and coordinating breaks for my mother was time consuming because it was difficult getting her in and out of the car. My mother noted that I did all the driving, but that Blake was directing the navigation despite the fact that Google Maps was doing all the work, and anyway I had done this drive many times before. Twice while we were driving to my mother's house, I caught Blake pulling on a tooth. I chastised him and asked him to stop. He seemed to leave it alone, at least when I was paying attention. I have a feeling he was doing it more discreetly.

We spent one night at my mother's house to recuperate and helped collect her things. We shut the house down for an extended period. Blake had asked me to open all the windows to air out the house for some reason, and then I was to close them before we left. I ended up missing one in the laundry room. Blake went around to check, then yelled at me for missing it.

The next day, we continued by driving north, far upstate, where Blake grew up, but it was snowing. While this made our journey more difficult, the road crews were doing a good job of caring for the highways. At some point, Blake took over driving, insisting he was the better snow driver. My mother recalls Blake complaining about his tooth a few times on the second leg of the drive.

She also remembers meeting Blake's family and getting along wonderfully; our mothers were chatting and laughing, enjoying each other's company. My mother also got to meet Blake's sister and her fiancé at his mother's brand-new bakery. Blake's mother was getting to live the dream of her life by opening this new business; it was a delicate time because it had not yet established a regular trade and she had to go into debt to open it in the first place. In a small town, forming a bad reputation straight away will destroy any chance of your small regular customer base from returning.

We drove to Lake George and then into the beautiful snow-covered mountains. Blake stopped at a church where he used to play the pipe organ. He talked someone into letting him play several songs for us. He was an astonishing organ player. My mother will never forget the music he played that day. His grandmother later told her that many people used to come to Sunday sermons just to hear him play.

We also stopped at a liquor store. The clerk squealed in delight when she saw Blake. He was probably a frequent customer when he lived there. I don't recall much about it, but my mother noted the tension between us later. We ended up moving on and enjoying some wine together in the hot tub at my mother's hotel. She remembers this as the last good part of the trip. Blake got quite drunk that evening and we had a fight. Everything blew up from there on.

We were due to leave early the next morning and Blake had made a big deal about the ribs he was going to cook for a gathering of his extended family at his mother's bakery on our last evening together. He was really selling it and being dramatic. He was to cook in her commercial kitchen, and he planned for the group to eat together in the restaurant, which was closed to the public.

We had planned everything for a perfect evening meal and our trip home the following morning. Blake was complaining about his tooth all day. It became more frequent the closer we got to dinner. It was causing his mother a lot of angst because they had to host their family members after working in the bakery all day.

About twenty minutes before the ribs were done, Blake's other root-canal tooth came out. He wailed in pain initially but said he would continue cooking, like a trooper. He grimaced in pain. I was tasked with frantically calling dentists on what was the Saturday evening of Thanksgiving to figure out what to do. His relatives glared at me. He had already told them that I'd punched his teeth out in a fit of rage and so they blamed me for what had just happened. Even though this went unmentioned, it was communicated with accusatory stares.

Blake continued to work diligently through the obvious pain. He was absolutely devoted to cooking his meal. I eventually found a dentist who prescribed pain meds as a stopgap measure, just as the ribs were finally being served. I wolfed down two ribs and went off to get the pain medication; it was the best we could do on the evening of Thanksgiving. For the real deal, it would need to wait until Monday, so we agreed we might as well drive home and find a dentist back there.

My mother describes the evening as having had a pall cast over it by Blake's medical issue and everyone was stressed about it. She was told by another relative that Blake had not only been a difficult child but also a troubled teen. He caused a lot of problems at school that required frequent parental intervention. Apparently, a counselor informed the family that Blake had some kind of personality disorder, but nobody mentioned which one.

The family expected the following day to be busy because there was a major town shopping event planned, one that would make or break the new business. They were very concerned that Blake's issues would cause problems at the bakery at a very critical time. He was driving angst in his close family the same way he had done with me. Someone can be in pain and have medical issues without purposely destroying the emotional state of those around them. It's difficult for everyone, but less so if the sick person doesn't make everything a dramatic roller-coaster ride. That probably was the point. If Blake caused as many problems as he could for his mother's business and she failed, he could blame it on me for causing the tooth issues in the first place. It was unlikely he would not feel actual guilt about what he had done to his mother.

As soon as Blake and I were alone together, he spent hours degrading me. Once we were in his mother's upstairs bedroom, he did it quietly so that neither his mother nor grandmother, sleeping downstairs, could hear. He was a rabid animal and unleashed a tirade of abuse as he rehashed his claim that I was to blame for his teeth. Experience told me to ignore him and I said nothing except as expected. He kept going until one o'clock before finally announcing we could go to sleep. He turned over and immediately fell asleep. I meanwhile had been driven crazy by his actions but completely relieved for it to be over.

He continued, more intensely in the morning. All he'd had were pain meds, and they took time to take effect, so his outburst was likely driven by his pain. I knew I was now the only driver and that I had to get us all the way back to Ohio that day. I stared at the floor, the wall, anything that meant I didn't have to look at Blake. Finally, I couldn't take it anymore and snapped. I screamed at the top of my lungs, not caring if his whole family could hear.

"You can't talk to me like that. There is no way I can drive all the way to Ohio today if you keep at it."

I stormed downstairs, and his mother and grandmother looked terrified of me. It was clear he had told them the same lie as the rest of his family. I pretended nothing had happened and had a calm two-minute conversation with them. I was later told they were flabbergasted that they heard me scream at Blake upstairs and then had come downstairs and pretended nothing was going on.

Everyone was tense when Michelle arrived in a cab. We piled into the car and left to get my mother from her accommodation. I should have insisted Blake stay with his family. He was visibly in pain, irrational, and unstable. This would, of course, have led to the destruction of his mother's bakery because that is what he was good at: creating as many extra problems as he could to keep everyone busy.

On the way to my mother's, Blake started berating me again. It was insignificant compared to what he did in private, but he carried on right in front of Michelle. She immediately objected to what he said and told him it was inappropriate. I then said forcefully, "I can't possibly drive while you drill-sergeant me."

He immediately and permanently directed his unsavory words to target Michelle. She had interfered in his marriage by ever so gently telling him he shouldn't degrade and threaten me. He spent the rest of the day exacting revenge on her for this, needing to establish that if he wants to abuse someone, it's his prerogative. It also shuts down future challenges to his dominance before they happen by using extreme punishment for minor transgressions that are delivered in a semi random manner.

He became respectful and almost sweet with me. At the time, I suspected he bought the argument that I had to focus on the road and needed to vent at someone else. Now, I suspect it was to highlight the divide between the absolutely horrible abuse Michelle was going to receive next to the completely reasonable treatment I was getting. The switch between the two was immediate and, in retrospect, an obviously conscious decision. At the time, I was too exhausted and focused on our immediate needs to think of things so deeply.

I must have dropped Blake off somewhere before picking up my mother from her hotel because I had to leave both my mother and Michelle at the bakery to go get Blake. I don't recall this part of the day, but my mother remembers sitting for four hours at a table in the tiny bakery during its very critical commercial holiday, waiting for us to arrive. Eventually, Blake's brother-in-law (who was working behind the counter) kicked them out because he needed the table. My mother couldn't stand the idea of being pushed by Michelle through the cold snow in her wheelchair, so they went into the kitchen area with Blake's mother, the cook. My mother's memory is of feeling very awkward and being in the way.

I have not forgotten arguing with Blake about finding a dentist in upstate N.Y. versus driving back and getting one back home. He became resolute that I find one right away on Thanksgiving weekend. I was absolutely confident there was a zero percent chance of that happening, that it would have to wait until Monday or Tuesday, and that I needed to be driving back to Wisconsin immediately so I could make it to work on Monday. I couldn't take an entire week off by not even starting the trip home and I certainly couldn't abandon everyone in this state and leave early.

After much calling around, I proved that none of the few dentists in the twenty-five-mile region of the small town we were in could accommodate Blake until late the following week. After two phone calls back home, I found an emergency dentist who could fit Blake in on Tuesday. Now we had to drive back there quickly to make the appointment. We picked up my mother and Michelle, much to the delight of Blake's family, who were happy to see everyone leaving. They could focus on their own lives again in the bakery and not be distracted by Blake's extravagant drama.

He took several of the painkillers I had procured for him and went to sleep in the front seat while I used the GPS to navigate. It ended up directing us around some traffic along a different route than Blake had suggested we take. When he woke up, he was irate that I wasn't on the expected route and screamed at me. I calmly explained the GPS was directing me, so why would I take the slower route? That was when he decided to continue punishing Michelle for her earlier transgression of protecting me from unreasonable treatment. He even threatened to drop her off in a random location in Pennsylvania, a prospect that terrified the poor woman.

My mother and I sat aghast in the car heading west as he destroyed Michelle for hours. My mother, like me before her, could not completely recall the abusive words hurled around her for hours. Somehow, our brains couldn't remember specifics with such a torrent. We eventually shut down and acquiesced to anything he wanted. I needed to support Michelle, but I was too afraid. I couldn't take any more myself. It wasn't long before the innocent and sweet child-like woman was in tears. Far away from her family with no sense of self-dependence, she was reliant on us to get her back home and care for her.

Eventually, I had to intercede. I couldn't sit by and let this happen. He directed nastiness at her, and then I tried to distract him with pleasantries and tell him to leave her alone. If it was a small comment, I'd let it go. If it went on for more than a minute, I'd shut it down. I knew I couldn't stop what was happening, but I was reducing the pain when he really crossed the line. He was affording me a small amount of control.

We were traumatized by the time we stopped in a crowded rest area in Pennsylvania; it had been maybe two hours of Blake abusing Michelle and me trying to distract him. I made it clear that we needed to keep this efficient because I had to drive all the way to Ohio alone. Michelle begged for ice cream. She needed emotional comfort, and while I certainly wanted her to have any that was available, there was no way I was going to wait around while she ate it. I told her she could eat it in the car, despite knowing she would drop the entire thing on the car seat within minutes of having it. I was past the point of caring.

While I wheeled my mother into the building with Michelle in tow, Blake waited in the car. We walked in to see a massive queue of people in line for the only restaurant. I was focused on helping my mother get to the bathroom and didn't think about it. Mom said she wanted to make her way to the restroom herself, and I let her go ahead from the front entrance. Michelle, noticing there was no way she could get service in ten minutes or less, came up with a plan. She burst into tears.

We were standing just inside the door, with maybe forty people about ten feet away watching us and another fifty people in the seating area to our left. Michelle had her back to the line, and I was watching them all watch us. She cried loudly about the way Blake was treating her and made it clear to the entire room that she was being verbally abused. They watched in awed silence as this woman, who was clearly unrelated to neither my mother nor me, acted beholden to us.

I heard someone say, "I wonder whose relative *that* is."

I decided I had better explain myself to the room. But I pretended to be explaining it to Michelle as loudly as I could.

I said, "There is a drill sergeant in the car and his tooth fell out. I have sixteen hours of driving left, all by myself. He is in a lot of pain. Don't interact with him. Interact with my mother and me only. Try to stick with my mother to separate the front seat from the backseat. Ignore him when he goes off. Tune him out. I can't do anything about it other than distract him as best I can the way I already have been. I could also drop you off at an airport."

She stepped forward, her lip quivering, and blurted out, "No, please don't! Don't leave me alone in a public place, I don't know. Please! I'll take the ride with you. But... the ice cream line is too long. Please, can't I have ice cream?"

Apart from her trembling, I could hear a slight sobbing in her voice. This was Michelle at her finest working for that ice cream, which I otherwise would not have been willing to wait for. Looking over at the line of people I saw, without exception, that they were staring at us.

I said loudly, "You know, I bet these nice people will just let you cut."

I gestured toward the line as the entire crowd murmured, "Yeah, go ahead."

Multiple people waved her toward the counter, and she walked right up to the assistant. I don't know if the worker charged her or not. It wouldn't surprise me if the ice cream was just handed to her.

When I emerged from the bathroom, an Indian man approached me. He was a dentist. My current plight had moved him and he wanted to help me. He said he would provide a dental service that evening: not to help the guy in the car, but to help me.

We took the address to his practice and piled into the car. Michelle spilled her ice cream, and Blake started to scream at her about it, but I wouldn't have it and stopped him. No drama over what I knew was going to happen. I couldn't have cared less about anything but keeping it quiet. Blake was respecting me, so I told him to ignore Michelle and only interact with me.

We got to the dentist, and I introduced him to his patient. The three of us waited in the front, and he got to work on Blake's mouth. We were going to do the billing, and he briefly considered charging us but ultimately decided against it. We were a charity case. I thanked him profusely and meant it.

We piled into the car and a different emotional scene unfolded. The active fire had been removed from Blake's mouth. We were all briefly hopeful it would end the tirades. They became less frequent, but he simmered in a quiet rage. It felt like a toy had been taken away from him. He could no longer use the lack of medical care as a cudgel against me. He stayed pleasant toward me for the rest of the trip.

He seldom interacted with the back seat but was a perfect angel to me. Now and then he would say horrible things to Michelle. I decided this was likely to continue, so I did my best to resolve things. If there was a tirade brewing, I shut it down, but if it was just a quick comment, I let it go. We mostly rode in what I can only describe as a terrified and deranged silence. You could cut the tension with a knife. I tried to focus on the road.

Incredibly, we made it to Ohio in one piece and settled into my aunt's house for the night. Blake continued to abuse Michelle in front of my aunt. She was horrified by his behavior but too afraid to say anything. She had taught and practiced psychology, working with deranged children for quite a while, and eventually likened Blake to those children. Later, she described him as a manipulative narcissist with Machiavellian tendencies. Machiavellian is a reference to a sixteenth-century Florentine philosopher who waged wars and said, "The ends justify the means."

We left my mother in Ohio and continued west. Our journey was largely silent. The evening's rest after his procedure must have reduced his pain and calmed him down more. Michelle and I were both too afraid to say anything and remained quiet. I would respond to anything Blake said in the most direct, simple, and calm way—whatever made him happy. His sour mood filled the air, sucking all good energy out of the car and replacing it with constant fear.

As we drove through his favorite city, Chicago, his mood suddenly improved. No words were spoken, but it was like a huge component of horror had just lifted. As we headed out of town, he tried to make up with Michelle. She refused to listen. She was not going to forgive him for the abuse she had endured for so many hours and made it clear this was the last time she would ever speak to us.

We finally arrived home late Monday evening and dropped Michelle off. She stormed into her condo. I went back to work on Tuesday. I then had my evening class until nine o'clock. Blake made it to that emergency dental appointment to finish up whatever the angelic dentist who helped us enroute had started.

17. An Intolerable Life

I suppressed the trauma and moved on as quickly as I could. Things became buried in my subconscious because, deep down, I knew what was going on but was unable to face it. It was too scary, and I didn't know what to do about it. I became withdrawn but played the part Blake wanted and was the ghost in the painting of the two of us. I also knew that he wouldn't last long without me. I still cared for him despite everything, and he needed me to survive. It wasn't so much the suicide threats; it was knowing his instability would lead to his own destruction. He needed a stabilizing factor, and I was as close as it could possibly get. Any decision to leave would be a decision to let him die. And I loved him too much to let that happen.

Things improved. Blake cooked fancy meals, and we romanced even if we made little actual love. Instead of our usual two bottles of wine each night, we were now opening a third bottle and enjoying our time together in a constant drunken stupor. A fair amount of good wine would go to waste. (After all, it wasn't Blake's money.) I honestly couldn't drink a full bottle, and initially I felt sick about three quarters of the way through; Blake would continually pressure me to drink more, but eventually my nausea prevented me. Our life together was frequently full of excitement and chaos. The decisions made were haphazard, chaotic... and frequently fun.

My double life continued as I emerged as one of the primary cores of my team at work: the framework for everything was my development. I had designed and authored everything related to the patient portal. I was effectively acting as system architect, developer, and support. A steady stream of people came to me for advice and decisions related to our application.

I was also a social center and provided entertainment for the team when we got new employees. We had a fresh recruit, and a particularly goofy quality assurance specialist (QAer) would ask humorous questions to get everyone to know each other a little better. We found out the new employee had gone to my college, so he asked me if I knew him and what his nickname had been in school. I clearly indicated that I had not known this person, but the QAer pressed anyway.

"Okay, so what would his nickname have been if you had known him?" somebody asked.

I came up with a funny idea and decided to share it.

"Okay, I'm just making this up, but his nickname was pudding-butt."

I then paused, giving people a chance to absorb this horrible but funny moniker and start making assumptions about what it meant. A few girls reacted with disgust, and there was a brief off-topic conversation to boot, giving it time to really sink in. This was when I noticed the poor kid was crying. Major *oops*. I continued my story, "Well, again I'm entirely making this up, but he had sat in pudding on the first day we were all at lunch. The whole cafeteria saw it, so everyone started calling him pudding-butt as a joke."

Fortunately, the kid started laughing pretty hard about this, but it was still clear he had been crying.

One of the ladies interceded, "Was it *chocolate* pudding?"

Her tone of voice indicated this was not acceptable, so I thought about the funniest color. "No, it was banana, or possibly lemon flavored. I'm not sure, it was bright yellow. Lemon is the brightest yellow, so let's go with that."

Everyone laughed. Someone inquired, "Why is yellow so funny? Brown would not have been funny at all, but yellow was really funny."

I replied, "Because it was unexpected." I felt bad at this point though, so I continued trying to undo the damage my joke had caused. "He actually became really popular because of it. I think the guys just liked saying things like, 'I hung out with pudding-butt last weekend,' and so it became a competition to get him to go to their party or just hang out. He was super popular. Even the ladies got in on the action, from what I heard he was getting laid all the time and never heard any complaints about, er, his performance or whatever."

A few girls in the room seemed upset by all this, calling it "crude" and "disgusting." The person who assigned me the task said, "But that's what a college nickname is! He got the assignment perfectly."

I still felt I had gone too far and decided to avoid participating in any future "hazing."

As Christmas approached, Blake insisted I take another class. He wouldn't take no for an answer. My manager didn't understand why I wanted to take it, but again he approved. I continued to be constantly busy with school and work, giving Blake the free time he wanted. Meanwhile, my alcohol tolerance had increased, and I was probably drinking up to a full bottle of wine. At least I was consuming it instead of dumping a bunch down the drain.

In the lead up to Christmas, we were both on break from school. Blake was spending time with a very cute nineteen-year-old who went by the name of Talon. He described Talon as homeless, although the kid had a bedroom in a house on the far side of town. He worked at the bakery around the corner from our condo, which was much more conveniently located for his work because he relied on public transit. Blake told me it was a non-sexual love affair. He wanted Talon to move in and sleep in the extra bedroom with his fiancé, who had his own place but would likely stay over sometimes. I didn't really want to go along with the idea, but didn't want to fight with Blake, so welcoming our new guest happened fairly quickly. I figured an outside observer might help reduce the torrent of abuse that occurred in private.

The two of us started to spend time with Talon, but he was clearly Blake's friend and not mine. They would spend as much time together as possible while I was at work and frequently went out without me. They became incredibly close emotionally, and Blake openly admitted he was having an emotional affair with the kid, going as far as saying he was in love with him but still claiming they weren't having sex. Talon was snide and had an extremely high opinion of himself, given that he washed dishes for a living and had no place to call his own. He spoke derisively about others he knew nothing about.

The three of us were leaving a restaurant when a well-dressed black woman walked by. She could have been a CEO. Talon made a sick racist joke about her that had no basis in visible reality. Blake and I were both aghast. It became just another trauma for me to suppress.

Back home, Blake made sure Talon knew his remark was unacceptable, but I regretted not lambasting him right there in the street, so that woman had her well-deserved dignity restored.

Talon later told Blake a horror story about rape parties he attended. He said the bartenders drugged the intended victim, and there was a cop stationed outside the bar. If the victim managed to escape, the cop would bring them back in to make sure they couldn't get assistance. The police were a honeypot, pretending to be a beacon of hope for help, but acting as a final snare.

Talon said it had been going on for twenty years and that he had attended several in the last few years. They generally targeted women who were unlikely to be believed, but he was on good terms with the coordinator and could arrange for someone to be the victim by special request. I guess there's no need to worry about checking identification for teenagers if you are throwing a rape party in a bar with police assistance.

I wasn't sure if it was true, but it horrified me. My perspective of the city began to warp slightly. It no longer felt like a peaceful place. I wondered who the rapists were, other than the one already living with Blake and me.

We continued to live what I can only describe as a slightly insane life as school started back up again. It was full of fun, adventure, and inebriation. I had crazy hours and was exhausted most of the time. I had no emotional outlet. I was cut off from the world but living in it and not allowed to have a say. There was no one to talk to about what was happening. Most events were pushed into my subconscious as I prepared for the next onslaught.

At this point, I was driving background anxiety without necessarily being aware of it. I started to hate my life. For me to lie down and give up would have let Blake continue with whatever the heck it was he wanted to do and use my credit card to his heart's content. I couldn't fight.

Blake would go out to the bars with Talon during the day. He would be drunk by the time I got home. I'm not sure how he was juggling his school with all his bar time. They spent every hour together and became almost attached at the hip. Talon's fiancé would stay over sometimes, and that was helpful to separate Talon and Blake. Talon had no sense of decency or morality. He was fashion-focused and very much lived on the surface of life without any depth.

Eventually, the cracks showed, and I became so low that I decided to try an antidepressant. The pills didn't take effect immediately, but after about four days, I felt different. Fortunately, that was a Friday. My emotions woke up and became incredibly intense. I suddenly felt terror so profound it consumed me. I didn't understand where it was coming from, but in retrospect, it was my fear of Blake being reawakened. Tension and fear were constant and highly magnified.

I entered a super alert, terrified state just as a large project for my class was due. I knew I needed to work on it over the weekend, but I could not focus on the computer due to the effects of the medication. For some reason, I took another pill Sunday morning when I should have stopped or skipped a dose. On Monday, I stopped taking the medication and, for the first time in months, put my foot down with Blake.

"I absolutely have to spend every possible moment after work on the class assignment. It's due by midnight, and there's a slight chance I can get eighty percent of it done in time. Probably not, though."

I left for work with the car.

When I got home, Blake said he had just gotten back from the bar. It was time to punish me for attempting to assert any form of control over my life. He started criticizing me about not cleaning up and said it couldn't wait.

"I haven't got time," I told him. "I need to finish this project by tomorrow and building a new programming language compiler from the ground up is not something you can do in a single evening."

That made no difference to him, and he began one of his long rants. I tried to ignore him and start my project. This incensed him, and the argument became about a lot more than cleaning. He gaslit me as the drill sergeant for three and a half hours. Next thing, he stood in front of me.

"Okay, you can start your project now. Bye sweetie, I'm going back to the bar."

I looked at the time; it was nine o'clock. Exhausted from the screaming, I gave up on the project immediately. I collapsed on the couch, completely spent.

I was overwhelmed and drugged up enough on antidepressants to do what needed to be done without regard for the consequences.

18. Yanking Out the Parasite

About an hour later, I terminated our relationship by text. Some would say it was a coward's way out, but I realized I was too afraid to face him. I needed out because I was so frightened of him, and at least once I had sent it, the deed was done. It was a long text message. There was no room to think about what the consequences would be. He needed to be out of my life. The strange mental health state the antidepressants had engendered in me certainly helped. They had magnified my fear so much that it couldn't be ignored any longer. The numbness I had developed to his shenanigans was suddenly gone. My love didn't matter. Constant suffering for it and letting him destroy me simply wasn't worth it. I had to protect myself.

Doing it this way was fine because if he had been sitting in front of me, it would be hours of degradation followed by sweet talking to get me back. We had been down this road many times before. He was in the bar then and would likely become enraged upon reading my message.

However, it would make him the center of attention, which is what he always wanted. He would get it out at the bar, everyone would be sympathetic because what kind of asshole breaks up with his husband by text? They couldn't possibly know that I lived in fear of the psychological trauma caused by his long emotional fits or that I remembered almost being strangled to death and having every attempt I made to defend myself used against me, turned into yet another tool used to try and destroy me. They would have no idea that there was a monster hiding under the surface of his confident, friendly exterior. They couldn't know that he had threatened death and continuous suffering if I left or that he would bring up suicide as a final cudgel as well.

The nice thing about this method, and the timing, was that his emotional turmoil would be so public that there was no way to take it back. He couldn't possibly beat me emotionally until I agreed to stay. We would be done. And this actually worked. When he came back, he was clear that my action had permanently terminated the relationship because of how public it was. The entire bar heard about what was going on. There was more fighting, and he started threatening me. He reminded me he had nowhere to go and no income now.

He said it was my fault he got kicked out of the army. I had cost him his teeth and his job. I was too afraid to argue with him and just let him rant at me; there was no point in even listening because anything I said would fall on deaf ears anyway and just extend the torment. I agreed to everything he demanded. He was going to stay in the condo and sleep on the couch. Talon would continue to sleep in the extra bedroom. I have no idea how long his ranting went on for, but I didn't get much sleep that night; I just listened and provided a very blank, "Okay" to anything that required my input.

Fortunately, Blake was almost immediately out of my life. He spent his time with Talon, or he was at the bars. They both kept odd hours and avoided me most of the time. He would come to me alone only if he wanted something from me. He almost sounded rational until I even briefly considered saying no. I would ultimately agree to everything, because I truly wanted him to be able to move on. As afraid of him as I was, I still loved him. I couldn't stand to be with him but wanted the best for him. I wanted him to have a future and knew I had to help provide it somehow—or it simply wouldn't happen.

He insisted I pay his bar tab, and I acquiesced without arguing. He decided I had to pay for his new apartment. I knew he couldn't afford one on his own. He couldn't possibly hold down a job. So, I agreed to his requests even though he was draining my finances with his bar tab. He was even buying other people drinks, so he could be popular at my expense.

I was prepared to do anything to keep the peace. Anything to stay alive. Anything to keep him alive. I was as frightened as I had ever been, both for myself and for him. I initially agreed to an $800-a-month cap for his rent, and he went along with that for about a week.

Shortly after, he insisted that the apartment had to be in Chicago. I was flabbergasted. I made it clear to him that there weren't apartments for $800 a month in Chicago; they were significantly more expensive. How was he going to live in that city without a source of income? Even if I was providing the apartment, there was no way he could survive without a decent job. That didn't matter though. I had to pay for it, and he wasn't going to take no for an answer. The harassment continued until I agreed. I did actually try this time; at least in part, because I knew there was no way he could make it work, even with me paying the rent.

Everything else I had just immediately given into in order to make him happy. I thought perhaps he wouldn't publicly smear me if I did. I thought perhaps he could move on civilly or build himself a decent life. This was a fool's errand, though. He was vengeful to his core, and there was nothing I could have done to make him civil. Fundamentally, he was erratic, and there was no way he could maintain a stable state long enough to hold decent employment. He would never be willing to do what it took to keep a job. The first time someone did something even remotely inappropriate, he would explode all over them and get fired for it.

It didn't take long for him to find an apartment this time, certainly not when I was the one paying, and it was a place he was motivated to live in. We traveled down together so I could sign on the dotted line, agreeing to $2,000 a month for an entire year. There was no way I could afford it, but it didn't matter. It was set to begin in the early summer after Blake graduated college. This left several months' gap between his officially leaving our shared condo and the beginning of his new lease. He indicated he could easily couch surf and became civil and friendly again, helping me maintain my illusion that giving him what he wanted would somehow keep him from destroying me.

Not long after, Blake got kicked out of college. His adviser had told him some hard truths, and Blake didn't like it. I wonder if they had decided he needed to repeat a semester and Blake refused to accept it. I do not know what he said or how aggressive he'd become, but Blake was permanently out, and according to him, it was his adviser's fault.

The funny thing is, this was the same man who had gotten Blake into school in the first place and coached him throughout. He had never had a bad word to say about Blake before, and I can't imagine he would want to invest all that time, only to terminate the relationship early. Blake probably threatened or tried to blackmail him in some way.

Nevertheless, it was a devastating blow for Blake. But of course, he deflected the blame onto me and said it was my fault because I wanted a divorce. He said this had affected his mental state and that I was incredibly selfish for being unwilling to wait a few more months before collapsing under the weight of his abuse. Meanwhile, all I had asked for was one pre-committed evening to finish my school assignment. From me, it was always give and never receive.

Blake was still present in the condo, but not often. He told me he was couch surfing, and he somehow convinced Michelle that the abuse she suffered at Thanksgiving was all my fault and made it up to her somehow. I believe he was on her couch. Her memory had probably faded some, and Blake could use his manipulation skills to honey-tongue his way back into her life. He needed her now as a regular crash pad after all, and she lived two blocks from his favorite bar. I do not know how he got her to forgive him because he never discussed it with me.

Blake talked me into letting Talon stay in the extra bedroom after he left because of how convenient my place was to Talon's work, and I eventually relented. I was far more interested in getting rid of Blake than anything else.

The end of Blake's last month living with me was finally approaching. We were on the homestretch. Blake made a big deal out of having dinner together in a lovely restaurant the night he officially gave me back his key. It was going to be a few days early. He wanted Michelle to join us for dinner. I don't really know why, but it was probably because he was crashing on her couch, and she simply wanted to come along. I was happy to have a witness present. Blake gave me his copy of the key to the condo at home before we went out, then we met Michelle at the restaurant.

After a pleasant dinner, we had a couple of drinks, and everyone was in excellent form. Blake appeared to have fully accepted that it was over between us. He even discussed his future. And in a totally innocuous comment, I mentioned that we should both move on and, who knows, I might find another partner in time.

I couldn't believe his reaction to my meaningless comment. Consumed with jealousy, he was clearly triggered and flew into a rage. He screamed and yelled and berated me as we left the restaurant. It continued as we made our way toward the car, which was parked past our favorite bar a few minutes away. He calmed down a little as we approached the bar and said he was over it. He apologized and suggested we go inside.

The bar was packed. Blake immediately accused me of cheating on him years ago in a voice loud enough for everyone to hear. He wanted a public fight. He needed to humiliate me in front of everyone.

Making for the door, I ran out. I should have stood my ground and made sure everyone knew about the things he had done to me, but I did not want a public fight. All this was more trauma for me. It was a wonderful dramatic show for him that gave him the spotlight.

I got home, collapsed onto the bed and went catatonic. I knew Blake would come back and continue, but I couldn't take anymore. He eventually showed up at the door but had previously given me his key. So he couldn't gain entry. He was pounding the frame and screaming horrible, violent threats.

'I'm going to tear your spine out and shove it up your ass.'

This is the one I remember most clearly, but his ranting went on for a while along similar lines. He sounded deranged and beyond furious.

In what had become a regular occurrence for me, being used to his abuse, I was totally resigned to what would happen next. I got out of bed and silently walked over to the door, unlocked it, and let him in. I walked back to the bedroom as he rushed in and started yelling at me. He had Talon with him. I ignored them both as I lay down in bed again, my eyes open and not moving. Blake continued yelling for quite a while, eventually becoming frustrated at my catatonic state. It may have been an hour, but he eventually gave up and left the room with Talon.

I immediately got up and went to the bathroom without thinking of locking the door again. Blake came right back inside at that moment and headed straight for me, claiming to want his toothbrush. I was too afraid to face him and felt trapped in the tiny bathroom. He was at the door wanting in, but I wouldn't let him.

I held the door shut and said, "No, you can't come in."

He had more strength than me and forced it open. I fell back against the bathtub and lay on the ground whimpering. Defending myself in any way was the furthest thing from my mind. He would simply use any attempts at self-defense against me in the future. I felt helpless and screamed at the top of my lungs, hoping someone else would hear.

This freaked Blake out, and he called 911. The police didn't stay long or provide any advice. I was told I could press charges, but I declined because the potential repercussions terrified me. I should have fessed up about everything, but I was too scared. It seemed like the police and ex-military were a club and that they were not going to help me. Deep down, I still wanted Blake to move on and have a decent life after me. There was no need to destroy him with this. But I should have. My better nature was being used against me.

Blake agreed to leave and not return. So did Talon, who had long made it clear that any police presence would be the last time he would be seen near the condo. Now I had my space to myself again, but Blake had the extra bedroom completely full of his possessions; he had not removed his stuff. He asked me to hang on to them until he was ready to take it all. The cat that never liked me remained, and Blake threatened to kill me if I tried to give it away. This took place at the beginning of spring, less than a year after our marriage. Blake's new lease in Chicago would not begin until early summer because it had been set up to begin after Blake graduated from the college he had been kicked out of.

This meant Blake was a lurking presence around town and provided him with ample opportunity to convince others to finish the murderous job he failed to complete.

19. Compel Others

I needed help but did not know how to get it. My idea that the police would take his side no matter what was deeply ingrained.

My job provided five days of sick leave a year but had to be used in four-hour increments. All the mental health counseling was in the middle of the day, so I was not able to pursue a private counselor without burning through the tiny bit of leave I needed when I was actually sick, required a medical doctor, or was dealing with the chronic issues related to my connective tissue disorder. The job's location was far away from all the healthcare providers, which meant I couldn't just leave for a brief period.

I wanted to block Blake on Facebook, but I was not able to because he had already blocked me; this enabled him to stalk me there. He could undo it anytime to check out my activity and then reactivate it without me ever knowing. I saw him around town now and then, but we ignored each other. He seemed to be shadowing me at times. I still felt intense fear anytime I spotted him. My stomach would churn, and I would almost puke, my heart did funny things, and I became dizzy. If I entered somewhere, and he was already present, I would run away. Or, I would try to ignore him if he arrived and I was already there. Sometimes I left shortly after he appeared. I started to avoid going out because I did not want to run into him.

My social ills and poor communication skills plagued me, as well as my self-conscious nature, due to differing slightly from others and having been through what I had experienced with Blake.

Meanwhile, Blake was going around telling people horrible and untrue things about me to poison the field and make it much more difficult. It also provoked sympathy for him, which seemed like an emotional necessity, while at the same time creating a wedge for me to get help from others. For a while, I was not aware that he was slandering me around town, but it slowly became clear that other people were out to get me. I had garbage thrown at me from a moving car several times. People started acting hostile, even at work. All of this left me depressed and lonely.

About a month after moving out, Blake and Talon convinced me to attend a party at the Inferno, a local club I had always wanted to check out. The venue was hosting a closing party. It was five blocks from where I lived, and they were giving away the last of their beer supplies before they tore the building down. I should have known better than to trust Blake. Especially after the story I overheard Talon talk about the rapes.

On the night of the party, I felt like going out to see this club before it was demolished. So, I showed up at the Inferno, and Talon was at the bar. He said something to the bartender before I ordered. I waited forever for my drink and watched other people get beers before me. I ran into someone I knew, a friend of Blake's I got along with. We started chatting. I relaxed and drank my beer.

Someone said, "Oh, it's a *guy* with the plastic cup!"

I became suspicious as I realized I was the only one with a plastic cup. I stopped drinking the beer at this point; it was mostly gone already. It wasn't long before I felt sick. I stumbled to the bathroom, but it was occupied so I sat down at a table and puzzled over what was going on. I wondered if my drink had been drugged. It wasn't even a full small beer. I shouldn't have felt so sick, but I wasn't entirely sure because I had stopped drinking almost entirely since Blake and I broke up. Also, I was prone to random, medically sensitive reactions. Remembering the story about rape parties I had overheard Talon tell, ones I didn't believe until that moment.

Suddenly, it dawned on me that this was exactly the same misery I had when I took GHB recreationally after the first break up between Blake and I. Fortunately, having taken it once before, the effects were slightly less pronounced. I was experiencing a loss of vision and dizziness. It was impossible for me to stand up, and my body desperately wanted to purge itself of all contents in a downward direction.

Sitting at the table, not making a scene or moving, I considered what to do. I decided the bartender had probably drugged me with GHB. The city was spitting me out of its gutter as retaliation for surviving someone who was much better at manipulation than I was. Later, something my grandmother said to me felt quite appropriate.

"People will believe any manner of crazy lies about a Jew without ever asking questions and use it to justify the most heinous of acts."

But I doubt being of half-Jewish descent was directly related to my experiences and that any minority group can experience something similar.

I noticed the guy at the door wasn't paying attention and decided it was a good time to walk out quickly and quietly. It was difficult to muster the strength to stand up and clasp the top of the plastic cup in my hand. If I extended the sleeve of my top, the man at the door wouldn't notice I was carrying anything. Looking straight ahead, I walked out, pretending nothing was wrong. I walked right by him, and it seemed like he hadn't noticed me. I raised no fuss, like everything was fine, and strolled to my car as my bowels howled with pain.

There was a cop car with its lights on, going into the parking lot. I sat in my car and tried to decide what to do while my mind raced. *That cop is here, just like Talon said in his story; he's a honey pot and if I go to him, he'll drag me back inside by force.*

I had a brief image of me injuring a bunch of the partygoers using my martial arts skills before I eventually collapsed, was tied up, and tortured to death as punishment for the initial damage.

It was only five blocks to home, not even a red light and probably no other cars. I considered calling 911 but couldn't work up the nerve. I knew I couldn't go to the cops. So, I drove home carefully, saw maybe one other car on the road, and parked directly in front of my condo.

I had agonizing pain in my stomach the entire drive. My focus was on getting to a safe bathroom. Leaning against the building's wall, I unlocked the door and stumbled inside, heading straight for the toilet. I spent the night alternating between lying in bed with intestinal agony and the bathroom. Eventually I slept most of it off.

Sunday was spent lying **around** in a slight daze, and I half slept most of the day and night. I'm sure I was affected on and off for another week, but I still made it to work on Monday and acted like everything was normal.

I eventually had a conversation with Blake about that night. He claimed to know nothing about it, but he later told me that as an act of revenge, Talon had set me up to be gang raped and beaten until I was disabled. Talon's mother had disowned him as a result.

At the time, I thought it wouldn't make sense for Blake to arrange this, as he needed me to find the money to pay for his apartment. So, he wanted me alive and employed. It's possible, though, that Blake manipulated Talon into setting this up so he could collect the insurance payout. I also don't know if Blake actually talked to Talon about it or if it was him manipulating me.

After several years, I did eventually report this to the local police, but the officer gasped and said, "Talon!?" in a concerned tone of voice when I reported his street name. He clearly knew the perpetrator and cared about him.

At some point around that time, I'm not exactly sure when, I was lured into a strange tourist attraction by a man on the street. They had turned off some giant industrial machine and were allowing tours of the inside.

I said, "Oh cool."

I was taken into a giant furnace room with two little girls who were visiting as well. While we were inside, an alarm went off because of some kind of accident. The machine was turning itself on and was going to incinerate the three of us. The woman operating the machine somehow saved me, but the little girls burned to death. I now wonder if this wasn't assassination attempt number three.

The first attempt would have been his strangulation. The second attempt would have been the rape party, as I suspect they planned to bury my body in the rubble of the building once it was torn down, but I don't really know.

I was trying to retain good relations and help Blake move on any way I could. Meanwhile, it looked like his plan was to kill me off before we were divorced so he could collect on the insurance and live large for the rest of his life. It appeared that even when Blake was out of my life, his tentacles reached far and wide; the toxicity of his persona manifested itself in others. He would never let me escape him. Failing to kill me meant he needed to make me as miserable as possible instead. He did this by employing a tactic similar to one used in war: salting the earth. This is when you sow literal salt into the ground as you retreat so the enemy can't later grow crops.

20. Salt the Earth

I found out that the city had support groups for survivors of domestic violence. There were two: one for gay men and one for women. In order to attend, you needed to be admitted first. The way to do so was to contact a particular police officer, so I gave him a call.

He told me Blake had already gone to the gay support group, and they were already biased against me. There was no way I could attend that group. The officer himself sometimes attended, and he had also been turned against me by what he had heard.

He did offer to get me into the women's group. The issue was that a male would not really be welcome because many female survivors of domestic abuse would not be comfortable with the presence of a man. It could affect their willingness to discuss private issues with me in the room. I would at best be a partial member and would frequently be asked to leave to give them privacy.

Additionally, I would need to walk in and immediately tell them about my problems without first being able to listen to the problems of others. It wouldn't be comfortable invading their space. I thought my perspective would be very different from theirs and wasn't really able to discuss my problems in the first place. I certainly couldn't do it with a bunch of strangers. So, I continued wallowing in the pain alone.

Eventually, Blake and another support group member (we'll call him Allen) approached me under the guise of helping Blake resolve his emotional issues and to determine why I had attacked him. I had met Allen before. The gay community is not very large.

"Hi. We've met before. My name is Allen in case you've forgotten, and I'm a member of the Trauma and Abuse Support Group. We're here today to help Blake resolve his emotional issues after your fight last year. We wanted to know why you attacked him," Allen said.

"Well, Blake had just tried to strangle me to death and—"

Blake immediately interjected with emotional force.

"Why didn't you tell me that happened? I don't remember that happening. You should have mentioned it."

I stood there dumbfounded while Blake took over the conversation. I'm not sure how long he spoke, as the words seemed to go in one ear and come out the other. They both left without me adding anything further. Blake was not going to allow me to share anything about the event. He needed as much of his side of the story to be retained by Allen. He could not permit me to mention the fact that he was enforcing his version using rhetorical violence or for Allen to potentially conclude that it had been a pre-planned action.

My desire was to move on and forget the entire experience. I focused on my job and tried to find joy here and there. I think I was slightly crazed at the time though—my mind was consumed by darkness. It was a difficult six months waiting for the divorce to be final. I met plenty of friendly people, but others were still being shitty. None of them had ever talked to me about their actions, and it felt random. I suspect I'm slightly on the Asperger's scale and have difficulty distinguishing people I don't know well. People asked weird questions at work, such as quizzing me in front of the entire team about whether I had ever raped someone.

I went out drinking now and then and recall someone walking up to me in the middle of the night and randomly punching me without explanation. This was offensive, obviously, but not a big deal for me at all as he punched me in the gut. The instant the fist makes initial contact, you tense your stomach muscles as hard as you can, and it causes you to bounce off it rather than get organ damage. I went flying backward and softened the momentum of the impact through a run. I did not hit them back or engage in any way.

To a degree, once violence has surrounded you long enough, it just finds you on its own. I visited Minneapolis and asked to see downtown with someone I had been staying with. He refused to go but said he would pick me up on the other side if

I insisted and strongly recommended against it. For some reason, I went anyway and discovered it was an entirely black neighborhood. This might not have been as off-putting to me as some, but the locals were giving me funny looks, and I did not know what they meant. I decided to put my hoodie up, so it was less obvious a lone 125-pound white man was walking around.

Although I certainly had no fear of anything that didn't involve a gun, it was just wiser to blend in as much as possible to avoid becoming a target or potentially needing to hurt someone to keep myself safe. I used the same sneaking ability I had employed to escape the bar the night of the attempted rape by looking straight ahead and thinking of nothing in my immediate surroundings, blocking everything from my mind as much as possible. I additionally grabbed some headphones and put them on to assist with blocking out the perception of others. This would give me an excuse to ignore anyone trying to interact with me for unknown purposes.

After walking a few blocks, I noticed a group of people gathered in a large square with thick sides around something unknown. It went from the wall at the edge of the sidewalk all the way to the other side of the street, with an empty section in the middle. I really wanted out of this neighborhood at that point, but there was no way around this crowd.

Without taking much time to think, I decided it must be a street performance of some kind. This was a stupid assumption given the context. I saw a single opening in the crowd along the inside of the square, where the sidewalk met the street. I avoided looking at whatever was happening to my left as I darted into the square with the intention of walking rapidly to the other side and escaping.

Shortly after I entered the square, my left shoulder told me a large, heavy object would shatter it, rapidly approaching my body from behind. My martial arts instincts kicked in and without even thinking, I avoided the object by rooting my right foot into the ground and swinging my left foot forward and to the right. This moved my shoulder out of the way and turned me toward my attacker. I merged my momentum with reaching toward the object using my left hand. I could see it was a metal baton and carefully made contact with it. Continuing my spin, I rotated the baton towards the holding thumb and pulled it forward; grabbing it from the hand of what I saw was a police officer. I had apparently just disarmed a cop.

I dropped the baton, and it rolled into a sewer. Pulling my hoodie down, I took off my headphones, revealing my white face. The cop, the only other white man present, was obviously completely shocked. We had a weird conversation where I had to convince him not to arrest me. In his words, I was not a member of a race of people that needs to be controlled.

Eventually, a member of the crowd pointed out that there was a dead body to my left. I was completely shocked and horrified by this. I looked around at the crowd and saw a perfect square of black people wearing what were essentially rags. They were standing at military attention, not moving and not speaking, but looking completely obedient and exuding fear. They were being brave though and wanted to observe the scene.

I looked at the cop. When I did, he took a step backward, and a combination of guilt and terror was briefly present on his face. He exuded fear from every pore; it seemed abundantly clear to me at this moment that the cop had murdered the person lying there and knew he had no real justification for his actions.

I had inadvertently cut through his crime scene. He was trying to keep it from turning into a riot and covering up his own guilt in broad daylight with any number of observers who would have been ignored by the courts as non-credible. I wish I had filed a complaint, but because I had taken the baton, I was scared. So, I just left and met up with my friend, eventually returning home.

Later that summer, I was standing in a park, when I saw a woman had lost control on some kind of wheeled device. She was about to injure herself and rolled right by me. Without thinking about it, I grabbed her, preventing her from being harmed. She thanked me for saving her life, but then she and her friends treated me like dogshit right there and then. On my way home, someone threw garbage at me again from another car.

I started to notice a pattern at work. Two developers had taken a dislike to me and were sabotaging me. One was blaming all his issues on my code, while the other was insisting that I inject terrible code into my work so it could pass his reviews. The programming he insisted on would break easily and didn't make any sense. His seal of approval was required, so the work got slightly twisted.

The company had a very blame-oriented culture, and these two developers were good at deflecting problems of their own making on to me. I tried to convince my manager I wasn't to blame, but he refused to look into it. I could potentially have done more about this but failed to get myself to focus on the problem, as the problems in my personal life distracted me.

Blake called the month before our divorce and said he was at Michelle's apartment and that she was in the background listening. Apparently, they were friends again, more evidence of Blake's incredible powers of persuasion. He told me he was giving up the Chicago apartment that he had made me sign a twelve-month lease for. The one that was bankrupting me and that I couldn't get out of. He was only two or three months in and wanted me to help him move back to town.

I told him maybe, but then he tried to convince me to spend the night at his apartment. I then clarified that while I was willing to consider helping him move, I emphasized that I would not stay the night with him under any circumstances. This evening together was very important to him, as he repeatedly tried to convince me to stay with him during the move. He tried several arguments, but I held my ground.

I eventually became irate and yelled at him. He put it on speakerphone so Michelle could hear me screaming at the top of my lungs, simply repeating what I had already said, but with greater force: I would absolutely not spend the night in his apartment. Never, ever would I be alone with him again. Then I hung up on him and ignored his repeated calls.

I reckoned he was planning to become a sweet, caring person and try to get back with me. I would not have it, but Blake figured out how to move back on his own. He was staying with

Michelle and had simply abandoned all the furniture I had purchased and that he had insisted on taking with him.

I was one of the first divorced gays in our state, one that didn't allow marriages yet. The judge and I discovered during the hearing that Blake worked in the courtroom cafeteria and handled his food. When the judge learned this, a brief look of shock and disgust appeared on his face. It appeared for less than a few seconds. My lawyer hadn't noticed. The judge quit shortly after that; it seems he had an issue ruling over a gay divorce. That one brief look on his face was the only indication I had of that during the proceeding.

It was kind of strange that Blake was working there as he had never done cafeteria work before and had even derided any work of that type in the past. His café job ended shortly after the proceedings. I believe he targeted a job at the court because he thought it would help him with the divorce somehow.

Once Blake's attempt to manipulate the judicial system failed, he decided to leave the city and move to Milwaukee. So, he unblocked me on Facebook and announced he had left town. For some reason, the app showed it to me. To celebrate, I went to what had been our favorite bar. There really were only a few gay bars, so no great opportunity to pick a new one. Blake spent so much time in bars that he had probably been to nearly all the decent ones anyway.

I walked in and saw him sitting at the bar with his back to the door. He was drinking and chatting with people. Quickly, I turned around without him seeing me and left. I almost threw up on the street on the sidewalk outside. I remember a woman watching me and I wondered what Blake was saying about me inside or had said in the past.

Blake left town shortly after, but beforehand he had to get a few things from the condo that he had left behind. Despite having previously agreed to give me notice of arrival, he didn't and was waiting outside my apartment with two police officers. He had told them I had abused him and that he was afraid of showing up alone.

Blake revealed he was leaving for Milwaukee the following day and needed his things immediately. I was pressured into providing instant entry. After some ado, he took hardly anything with him and left most of his possessions behind. I was left with the fear that he could show up again at any time.

After hardly any time at all, Blake contracted HIV in Milwaukee; apparently there is a very high rate of disease there. I have to wonder if he already had it when he was trying to get me to crash at his apartment and wasn't hoping to infect me. Fortunately, I didn't fall for it that time. In either case, this had soured his opinion of Milwaukee, so he was moving back to our city where the rents were relatively low. He wanted the rest of his possessions back but refused to come get them; he expected delivery. It enthused me to clear out the full bedroom his stuff was taking up, even though I was frustrated by the amount of work that had been fobbed off on me. We arranged a time, and I showed up at his new place to drop things off, but he was nowhere to be found; expecting me to wait around or something.

After a reasonable time, I started unloading the things into the yard. It was about an hour and half after our arranged meeting time when I abandoned it all in the yard. He called hours later, quite angry about what I had done. There was no appreciation for work that went into packing it all up and delivering it to him, or any apologies for not being available as scheduled. Just anger that I had made him move it all inside himself and had risked someone stealing it. It was a quiet suburban neighborhood, and no one had gone through anything. The only remaining direct remnant of Blake in my life was Mickey, the cat that did not like me and was still fighting with my cat on a regular basis.

I decided it would be safe to move on and came up with a plan to help me stay safe and provide emotional support.

21. A Cycle of Violence

Once I had extra space, I invited my cousin to live with me for a while. This gave me a sense of safety, having another person around to spend time with and not be an easy target. I met another interesting cast of local people; it was nice with a new set of energies around.

I connected with some people whom I still have fond memories of. A scientist who collected ice in Antarctica to study neutrinos; a teacher I developed emotions for, wrestlers, and an IT admin person. I learned about a hidden party scene and discovered raves.

I gave Mickey the cat to one of my cousin's friends under the condition that I could take him back to give to Blake in the unlikely event he could care for an animal. Very early on, there was a medical issue where I needed to pay upfront for the cat's veterinary costs and take him in myself. I didn't mind, but it raised some concerns.

My friend eventually repaid me for the vet costs and stabilized himself so that he could care for an animal. It probably helped transition him into the next phase of his life, but I'm guessing here.

In time, I learned that Mickey entered a gay relationship with another cat as the bottom and was living a happy life. I also found out while writing this book that he passed due to medical issues and old age.

I was active on Facebook, and someone was riling me as we approached the 2016 election. It was important to some group, whether the Republican Party or the Russians, that I be perpetually mad at Hillary Clinton. It was relentless, and I espoused that anger in my posts. I eventually realized I was being targeted with propaganda and tried to shut it down by unfollowing certain groups. Still, those groups would find me again and actively push their agenda at me. I eventually gave up on Facebook and deleted it because there was no way to avoid the constant stream of Hillary hate.

I voted for her, not because I particularly liked her as a candidate, but because I recognized Trump as a unique brand of evil, significantly worse than the others. Losing faith in the system, I stopped voting after this election. We have a choice between one brand of criminal that is kind of incompetent and the other that is outright evil, knows it, and is manipulating people in broad daylight.

I see the news. It feels more like they are bragging about the awful things politicians do than trying to shed light on horrors so we can do something about them. Often, it felt like a game where the two sides were playing us against the other to maintain control. It's advertising. Or maybe some rich folks were twisting things up.

One nice thing about the company I was working for is that it pays for a sabbatical once every five years to a country you have never visited. They would even pay for a friend to come along, so I planned an extended tour through several countries. For the first half, five of my college friends would join. The company was going to pay for the flight and hotel for the one least well off financially.

As Christmas approached, the CEO of the company decided our product needed to load data from multiple hospital systems and synthesize it for the patient. A wonderful choice for those needing it but incredibly difficult to accomplish. I had built these amazing tools in preparation for a big migration, and they were effectively ready for use: the perfect opportunity to jump in full steam.

We had nine months to rewrite everything, and we'd have to use all the various frameworks I had designed and authored. There was a demo due in one and a half months, while I was scheduled to be on sabbatical.

They tasked me with building the doctor/patient messaging system. I designed a framework to combine the messages from various systems and integrated it with other people's code to load the data. Two other content areas decided to use my list framework to display their results as well. I had to get it finished much earlier than everyone else because I was going to be away.

I warned my boss that this was a terrible idea and that something could go wrong. Who was going to fix it if something broke? I couldn't do anything if someone changed a dependency while I was away. I finished the system and left for my sabbatical. The other developers did not yet have a working product.

The first country we went to was Cambodia, and I met my friend group from college. We explored the country's rich and terrifying history. Tuk-tuk drivers operated as local cabs; some pedaled carts, and others had motorized ones. Everything was juxtaposed. I recall the power lines looking like people had attached their own wires. They were a gigantic mess.

The sense of hardship was strong, but the people struck me as hard-working and honest. It wasn't a creepy impoverishment where you sense predators looking for prey. I later got the feeling that punishment in Cambodia was extreme, resulting in the locals behaving themselves.

My friend and I were smoking a cigarette outside our hostel when a tuk-tuk driver shouted from the street, "Killing fields! Killing fields! You want go killing fields?"

My friend and I looked at each other in confusion.

The look said, "That man didn't seem to be threatening us, but that was extremely creepy."

We spoke about it a bit and then found out our guided tour was taking us there later. We learned about Cambodia's horrifying history and about the killing fields were where the Khmer Rouge had buried so many bodies at once that human bones rose to the surface. They had even made a tower of skulls from them, perhaps thirty feet high.

Some Cambodian citizens had studied abroad and decided to implement the holocaust back home, killing anyone who didn't accept their absolute authority and anyone with more intelligence or education than a simple farmer.

We also saw incredible ancient temples that were beyond fantastic, especially when considering how ancient peoples could have built them in a dense treacherous jungle.

Next was Hong Kong, though we technically had a hotel in southern China, as it was cheaper. We explored the island and the surrounding area, but I cannot say I got a good sense of the city. Things had a closed-off and slightly creepy vibe.

For some reason, we decided to spend Chinese New Year in Macau, a neighboring city. It was essentially the Portuguese version of Hong Kong that was returned to China earlier and had been fully integrated. We regretted this odd choice once we realized there was a parade in the Hong Kong area and we were missing it.

We later found out there was a massive riot during the parade due to police misconduct. So, we were fortunate. Macau was practically empty as a result, which meant that all the touristy things were easily accessible and not jam-packed with other people. Quite a few things were closed though.

My friends needed to leave; they couldn't stay for more than two weeks. I decided to go to the Philippines alone and randomly selected Cebu. I hired a guide for part of it. The highlight of my experience with her was scuba diving in MoalBoal, near the southwest part of the island. Right off the coast was a fantastical dense tropical rainforest of different fish, coral, and underwater plants.

I saw a nest of sea turtles. A smaller one was sleeping on the back of a larger one. There was a funny little imprint in the shell of the larger turtle that was just the right size for the smaller one, as if it nested on the larger tortoise frequently. I figured it was a baby, but I was later told that tortoises don't raise their own young. The family swam right by me after our presence slightly disturbed the nest. I also saw a poisonous lionfish, which the guide tried to warn me about visually, but I stared at it stupidly. It was beautiful and didn't bother us.

There was also a trip to a sardine run where I was surrounded by what could have been billions of small fish in all six directions (up and down included). The guide arranged to have her friend drive me to the airport, so I still had a few more days alone before it was time to leave.

I finished up my scuba certification and wandered the Cebu area. I met a local teacher on Grindr and we spent some time together. He took me to an old resort that had closed down. Apparently, it still had one of the nicest beaches in town, and locals used it in lieu of the tourist beaches. It really was beautiful and deserted. We climbed along rocks and found our own private area to snuggle by the waves and swim. We had a lovely, romantic time together.

When we were done and ready to head back, he told me that white people in Cebu had greater status than the locals did. Even if the locals were paying guests at the resorts, they still had a tendency to get harassed by the staff who assumed they were freeloading on their curated beach. He pointed out that we could walk back along the coast. The only issue was we had to cut through one of those resorts. He told me that since he was with a white person, we would likely get away with that.

We waded through a large sea marsh along the sand and took the shortcut through the resort. Sure enough, a staff member saw him walking ahead of me and went to yell at him. When I walked up and stood next to my friend, the guard looked surprised and backed off. He did not ask me for evidence I was staying at the resort (which was good, since I wasn't).

Right before leaving, I went to a dance club. I was curious about the local gay scene, so I decided to check one of those out. I arranged a round trip with one of the local drivers, Rocky, who my friend had been using. He agreed to take me to the Cebu City, where the gay clubs were and to bring me back in the evening. He also convinced me to get a massage at a local Filipino business and used his golf cart–like contraption to get me there.

It was too early to go out, so we were to head back to the hotel after my massage. I was surprised to find out that Rocky no longer had his cart. I was directed onto a public bus that stopped in the middle of nowhere about halfway back, where I was directed to get out so we could transfer. Shortly thereafter, we got on a smaller bus. I discovered this was a private vehicle filled with Rocky's family.

This was obviously fairly creepy. I became suspicious and slightly afraid. I considered whether I should jump off the bus and walk back. What if I was about to be the victim of homophobia again, or just another kidnapped tourist in the Philippines? I decided that I could take this crew in a fight if necessary. We were obviously heading in the right direction as I checked my map's application to verify. Rocky's mother introduced herself and, during the course of the conversation, made it clear she wasn't a homophobe. She seemed like quite a nice lady, and I had the impression the family would cause me no physical harm. I felt assured and they dropped me off at my hotel after a few minutes.

It wasn't until much later that I went out because clubs don't fill until late in the evening. I had taken a bit of a nap and packed up all my stuff before we left so I could come home fairly smashed, crash, wake up tired, and potentially still drunk. The plan was to catch up on sleep during the flight. I discovered that Rocky had rented a higher-powered golf cart; he indicated it was necessary for the longer trip to the city. We picked up his kind-of-cute young nephew along the way. They tried to pass him off to me; he wasn't gay but was open. I wasn't that interested and only wanted a safe space to dance in without getting harassed, so we took off to the clubs together.

We went to one place known for having sexy male dancers. It was briefly enjoyable, but that wasn't really my thing. I did have quite a few drinks before we headed out to a place that wasn't gay but was more dance oriented. I had become quite drunk and ended up paying for a bottle of something that I just shared with the driver and his nephew at our private table (everything was cheap anyway and he was just ferrying us around in a golf cart). The rest of the evening was spent on the dance floor, and I didn't need any more libation. The plan was to sober up slightly before I went to sleep. I also wanted to keep my wits about me, just in case.

Near the end of the night, the driver brought my cup to me, acting confused as to why I hadn't drunk anything. I took the tiniest sip, a thimbleful perhaps, and handed it back, not really wanting any more. Minutes later, I felt ill and rushed to the bathroom, which was fortunately unoccupied. This was only slightly different from my previous experiences with GHB.

Fortunately, my canary-like constitution saved me as I next spent long enough on the toilet to empty myself entirely of contents. I was done and recovering when security came to knock on the door because I had been there so long.

I could have easily left at that point, and fortunately I discovered Rocky waiting in the bathroom doorway, looking concerned. He quickly rushed me out of the club and back to the hotel. I had maybe three hours until I had to leave for my flight, which was taking off at 6 a.m. I was feeling ridiculously drunk (or something) for the entire ride. It would have made sense to have informed the club employee about my state. I was too out of it to protect myself at this point. Fortunately, my earlier evaluation that these people wouldn't hurt me proved to be true, and I was dropped off at my hotel.

After going into my room, I discovered that I couldn't locate my brand new $1,000 phone. I was so tired that I had to sleep, so I called the front desk and asked them to wake me as well as setting the in-room alarm. My guide's friend arrived at 4 a.m., as arranged, but I didn't hear a thing. I slept through the alarm, phone calls, and pounding on the door.

She repeatedly tried for thirty minutes until something finally roused me. I hurriedly did the final packing and left, still unable to find my phone. I went outside and found out she drove a motorcycle, and I was to ride behind her clinging to her for dear life, still drugged, as she rushed me to the distant airport.

Her hard work paid off, and we made it in the nick of time. She informed security of how soon my flight was leaving and they cut me to the front of every line; someone put me where I needed to be each time as I drunkenly stumbled around. I barely made it to my flight but can be thankful that my guide's friend worked so hard to get me to the airport! A woman judged me as I stood in line to get on the aircraft.

"Look how drunk he is. It's six in the morning. Americans, *hrmmph.*"

I almost shouted, "I was drugged and robbed, you judgmental bitch!" But I held my tongue.

I had to transfer in both Manila and Hong Kong: the former involves a taxi ride between airports. I was feeling much better by the time we got to Hong Kong. During the layover, I had time to recoup. I somehow sat next to the same woman on all three flights, although thankfully not the one who judged me. My phone never turned up, and I'm convinced that the driver had arranged things so he could steal it. They had decided not to kidnap me or hurt me but didn't mind robbing someone who was rich relative to them.

After clearing the poison from my body, it was then time to return to my poisoned city and career.

22. A Poisoned Career

I got back to work and was lambasted because the messaging was broken and didn't work for the demo. I investigated and someone had changed a dependency in a way that they knew required global updates and relied on the developers still present to adjust. It wouldn't even build. If someone spent five minutes looking at it, they would have figured it out because they had to make the same adjustments to their code. Exactly what I said would happen, happened. This was used as an excuse to give me less than a 0.5 percent raise.

The manager said it should not matter anyway because I was already earning top dollar. He said he confirmed with HR that this was the case. I found out what one of the other developers was making; I was at forty to sixty cents on the dollar or thereabouts despite being one of the primary cores of the team and the website's architect. But I had been there longer than this other person and absolutely contributed more to the team than he had. I figured maybe the company pays new people more, or other team members scapegoated me too much. The two developers I had problems with before blamed me for what were ostensibly their problems. There were multiple reasons. For years, I had been trying to do too much before Blake's and my divorce, and my ability to focus on my work had eventually degraded. I was in a hidden state of fear and trepidation.

I should have walked away from the company at that moment. They really needed me because I had written the frameworks for everything, and there wasn't any time to spare on their end. Instead, I acted out the same behavior I had engaged in when I was with Blake, but this time with my employer by not just quitting on the spot. I continued working for the people paying me scraps compared to my heterosexual peers. About two months later, they asked me to take over the entire 120-person team. I told them they had to pay me more or I wouldn't do it. Maybe I should have taken the job and assumed the raise would come. I'm not sure. Either way, that sort of terminated my career there. I was present but detached and off track.

Blake would call from time to time or appear in town for unknown reasons. At some point, he told me he had hung out with a blonde HR lady from the company I worked for. The company had a master list that ranked each of the developers who worked there and then adjusted salaries so they were in line with each person's ranking.

This blonde had worked for the company for so long that she had direct edit access to the ranking list. She would go in and unilaterally adjust the raise list to her liking. She wasn't supposed to do this but had been doing it for years anyway, internally justifying her actions as enforcing the culture.

Blake had lied to her, indicating I was terribly abusive, and punched his teeth out in a rage. The HR lady said she had already been stealing my raises for years anyway, but that she would accelerate the theft from then on. I'm not sure why she had been robbing me before, except to guess that it was anti-gay animus. Of all the bizarre and inappropriate questions I was asked during work meetings, hers were always the worst. They seemed to assume I preyed on children sexually, something I certainly have never done, nor do I have any inclination to do.

I brought this information to our HR department, but they were unwilling to investigate to find out who was involved. I didn't even have any idea how to locate this blonde, although I now suspect it was the same woman I saved in the park. Even though I reported this to the company, I got no response. Not sure I should have expected one since it only exposes them to liability.

I was deflated at work, knowing my salary differential from the others. I stopped performing and felt detached from the city in general. My inability to be comfortable in my skin definitely got in the way too. Whatever problems I faced seemed to fade eventually, but the scars remained.

I had been interviewing frequently, hoping to start over somewhere else. I was really too much of a mess to really pull it off, and I couldn't find anything that was exactly what I wanted anyway. In the end, I called an ex-colleague and asked him if his small company was still hiring. They were working in an area that was interesting to me, predictive AI, and I knew that he would recommend me for hiring; which would make the interview process much easier. They hired me immediately, and I prepared to relocate to Houston; it was a part of the country I had never really had any interest in. It didn't matter; anything to force a change.

I left the city alone and in shame. Despite everything that went on, I still have a hidden fondness for the town I was living in. It had started to feel like a home. But I became alienated from everything, and my emotions were suppressed or at least not expressed, so no one knew what had happened to me.

Shortly before I left town forever, there was a shooting outside my condo. It was just one bang, and the victim ran away with a minor leg injury. There was a huge cluster of people and an officer outside investigating. I was worried that a bad reputation would affect the price of condos in the area, but the sale went through, and I prepped to move.

Houston beckoned me in spring, about a year and a half after my divorce. I settled in and made some friends. A few months later, Hurricane Harvey hit, flooding the city for five days. They designed the roads to flood rather than the houses, so I was trapped.

I remember being confined in my first-floor apartment, worried my home would be next. I also remember having filled the bathtub with water in case the tap became undrinkable later. Fortunately, I did not need it. I think we mostly had power, but I don't recall. They eventually decided to flood the outlying areas, and people who had purchased houses in what were designated as floodplains learned why it was cheaper to build there.

One of my local friends drove a large SUV. He was coming to pick me up to get a meal at his favorite deli, so I had two breaks from what I had been making at home. I remained friends with this guy throughout my time in Houston; he was my barfly buddy. We would go to all the gay events together. He gave me a sense of safety after what happened at the Inferno.

Fairly early on in Houston, a well-dressed and agreeable-seeming black man approached me. He informed me that

Houston had a list. The intention of the list was to ensure that people in the big city look good and that I was doing reasonably well on that front. However, my hair was sometimes quite frazzled, and it would likely be impossible to maintain my long curly locks in the humidity of Houston.

He said they would add me to the list if my hair wasn't perfect at all times. He also mentioned that things had gone past being ignored, which was the original intention. People were starting to vandalize and assault people on the list, including desecrating their dead. I thought about this and realized I wanted nothing to do with any of that. He understood when I told him to add me to their list with a note indicating I was a dangerous person who they should not mess around with. I figured this would benefit me in two ways. I would not need to socialize with total jerks who engaged in this behavior, and they wouldn't subject me to their horrors.

Twice I heard about the note they had about me on their list. Once was from a man in a bar who looked me up and indicated the information he had told him I was dangerous and should be avoided. I told him that if he was associated with the people who desecrated the dead over awful hair and clothes that I wanted nothing to do with him. He said, "It seems like there has been a fundamental miscommunication, but I'm going to respect the information I have about you." He walked away.

The next time I heard about this list was when someone asked why a note indicating I was incredibly dangerous was there, and I told them what happened. They were shocked to learn I asked to have that added to my file. I recall saying they were despicable people for engaging in assault, vandalism, and desecration of the dead over hair and clothes. I made it clear that if they did that to me, I would become dangerous. That last part was said in my terror tone: a low, deep, growling voice, and then I spat at his feet. He reacted in shock and horror at that.

He might have thought, If you're that horrified by this, I'm sure others will be too. We have to rein that in. Perhaps I made a difference, perhaps not.

The younger hip crowd completely ignored me, but I formed a small group of mostly older friends, all decent seeming people. I had no respect for the behavior by the list people. There were lovely pool and beach parties I went to and a few concerts. I spent a lot of time at home playing with my new projector and on my computer. I generally had a good time. The people I interacted with were pleasant and seemingly decent people. My scary words had kept the list people at bay. Truthfully, in retrospect, I was not entirely reasonable during this time, and things could have been worked out with these folks. They were genuinely open to helping me, but I was not willing to negotiate with anyone or anything that had espoused violence after my experiences with Blake. I was also unwilling to share details about the horrifying past I wasn't even prepared to admit to internally.

I remember walking past an anti-Sharia-law protest. There were a bunch of idiots ranting against Muslims and a few manipulative people up front, egging them on. I entered the crowd and started spouting anti-Muslim nonsense to get their attention. Near the end of my rant, I shouted, "Down with all these stupid Stans, down with Pakistan, down with Afghanistan, down with Huey-stan." A country I just made up. I then started repeating, "Down with Huey-stan."

I heard the people up front said quietly, "We're losing the rubes." They were referring to the crowd.

The rubes were repeating, "Down with Huey-stan."

A black woman near the back said, "Was that a professional?"

I vanished.

The announcer said, "Where'd that guy go?"

From a distance, the crowd sounded different, and it made national news that there was an anti-Islamic protest in Houston and that they were chanting, "Down with Houston!"

A newspaper article even mentioned, "No, it was Huey-stan."

But no one bought it. I'm glad a riot didn't break out.

Blake disappeared from my life but would call. He made it clear that I had been his mark and that he had moved on. I knew he was shy about being honest, but he even broke into the truth here and there in little side comments.

His HIV was supposedly advancing to AIDS more rapidly than most and he had been bouncing around the country to various Veteran Administration Hospitals looking for decent treatment. It's worth mentioning that I'm regularly tested for HIV and am thankfully clear of infection myself.

I don't recall Blake ever discussing a plan for his future during our calls, at least not until our final phone call.

23. Final Conversation

It was in the spring or late winter about eight years after Blake and I first met. I was sitting on a step outside the large building I worked in at Greenway Plaza, smoking a cigarette. There was a football field–sized area in front of me where another large office building stood. My phone rang. The caller ID said it was Blake.

I answered the phone, and knowing it was him I very abruptly and rudely decided to avoid even saying hello. I instead said, "What do you want?"

He obviously noted my tone and knew I didn't want to speak to him.

"Now, I know you want nothing to do with me," he replied, "but I was wondering if you would be willing to narrowly discuss the topic of my death?"

I obviously had no desire to communicate with him at this point. Any words between us only brought up old traumas and triggered horrifying emotional pain. There was no way I was letting him know I still cared about him either. I didn't want to admit it to myself even. I felt frustrated and annoyed that I had to deal with his nonsense but was slightly intrigued by the idea that I might never need to deal with him again. Cautiously and with some of that annoyance expressed, I said, "Hmmm. I suppose."

He then dove straight to the heart of his cover story for calling. "My HIV infection is advancing more rapidly than most peoples, and I am going to die very soon. I'm preparing a list of people for the military to formally notify when it happens. Is that something you want? Do you want to be officially notified of my death?"

I immediately and without hesitation replied, "Yes. I would like to know."

Blake continued for a little while. I don't recall everything he said, but he was trying to explain why he was so sure he was going to die. He was blaming it on the rapid advance of his disease and claimed to be too far along and near death, but he sure sounded healthy. He had no weak qualities in his voice. It didn't make sense to me. Something didn't quite add up. He next got to the real purpose of his call. He wanted to know how I would feel once it happened and inquired, "I'm guessing you'll be just relieved?"

I decided to lie and said, 'Yeah, I'll just be relieved." It was the easiest thing to say. It's not that it was entirely untrue. I would certainly feel relief, but I would also be very upset by it. It was complicated. I had no idea how I would feel, but it would be filled with as much turmoil as our entire relationship had been. I still had love for him but couldn't let him know that. He'd want me to take him back and I would be willingly walking back into hell.

I mostly decided not to think about it as I left Blake to continue talking. He started to talk about what everyone else in his life would think about his death. His father wouldn't really care because he was a selfish asshole. It would garner some sympathy though. His sister would be relieved. He had been a constant thorn in her side since childhood anyway. His mother would have what I later found out was called complex grief, a bizarre mixture of relief and sorrow. His grandmother was the only one who would truly only be sorry that he was gone. He said he had always been good to her. He then said something about dying later that year, around Christmas. He casually mentioned that he had met someone who had two previous convictions killing someone in an act of rage.

Something finally clicked. I realized that we weren't actually talking about him dying of HIV. How could he know *when* he was going to die with such specificity? Why had he suddenly mentioned this other random person? I somehow knew that Blake was planning to manipulate the man into killing him. He wasn't going to die of HIV; he was planning to commit suicide.

A feeling of shock and horror so profound went through me that a man on the other side of the plaza saw the look on my face and started to literally run toward me. He was still on his way when I asked Blake, "Wait. Are you planning to manipulate a rageaholic into killing you as an act of suicide?" This was my term for someone who couldn't control their anger.

I sat there listening to Blake confirm my guess, my mouth agape. The random stranger arrived as I did that. Both he and Blake were speaking as I listened to them simultaneously. Blake was confirming my theory. He decided it didn't matter if I knew since I was going to be relieved at his death anyway. I wouldn't stop him, would I?

The random stranger, speaking while I listened to Blake confirming his suicide plan, said, "Man! You should have seen the look on your face! It was *so horrifying*; it was *hill-air-rious*. I saw it all the way from the other side of the plaza!"

The man stood there watching as I listened to Blake's horrifying tale. I must have looked shocked, horrified, traumatized, and somehow confirmed it to him without speaking. But I gave no indication I was paying any attention to him whatsoever. I ignored this random stranger and focused entirely on Blake.

The stranger said, 'Oh, wait, something actually horrifying is happening to you, isn't it?' I should have activated the speaker phone so this stranger could hear, but I continued to ignore him, completely enthralled by Blake's words. Eventually, the man stumbled backward three steps and wandered away. I never saw his face.

Blake continued, admitting even more of his plan. "I even set you up to die when it's over by lying to my old military buddies. I told them that story about you knocking my teeth out in a fit of rage and they are going to take care of you after I'm gone. They have actually tried a few times already. No one is entirely certain how you survived, but it seems they hadn't tried very hard. It's really going to escalate later."

"Yeah, I'm pretty hard to kill. My martial arts instructor really taught me some crazy skills, and I can survive things that would kill almost anyone else; you're far more likely to kill innocent people around me than succeed at killing *me*. Certainly, you don't want that do you?"

Blake said, "Surely by now, you must know I don't care about *that*?"

He was referring to killing innocent people. He then laughed maniacally. It was like all the masks he had worn for the duration of our relationship suddenly came off all at once. There was no need to lie anymore. He would be dead soon anyway.

The conversation only became more honest from there. I once spent time with a psychologist who worked with exceedingly difficult children. She didn't discuss their clinical interactions, but one child in particular had stolen her car and crashed it, as well as engaging in other highly aggressive and unacceptable behavior toward her. Years later, the then young adult had behaved as if they were old friends and acted like what she had gone through was actually old hijinks the two friends had engaged in together. They had entirely honest conversations, and this person had no understanding that these experiences were, in fact, traumatic for the psychologist. They were not friends, but this fact was lost on the young adult because of his narcissistic personality disorder. His reasoning seemed to be something like, *If these experiences were fun for himself, they must have been fun for everyone else as well.*

This final phone call with Blake reminded me of this child she had worked with. The primary difference was that Blake knew what he had put me through was horrifying. He knew he was manipulating me, as well as others. After all, he had been a trained professional interrogator working for the government. He had just suddenly decided to become honest. Perhaps it was knowing he was going to die soon. He didn't need to keep pretending. The long game he had been playing with me was seemingly already over in his mind.

Blake admitted that he had been trying to murder me the evening of the attempted strangulation so he could collect the insurance money. Also, he said he had pulled his own teeth out so he could tell others I had knocked them out in a fit of rage. He had been going around telling everyone I had been horrible to him during the relationship and painted me as a monster to garner sympathy and get things for free from others.

This brings me back to the spider that saved Blake before we met. In North America, we have the black widow spider. The female consumes the male after they mate. There have been a number of movies made about women who marry a man with the intention of murdering him so she can collect money; we call them black widows.

Blake had been planning to emulate the black widow so he could become one.

Until that phone call, I hadn't realized all of his behaviors were conscious. I had always assumed that he had emotional instability and that there was some kind of other personality that would take over during times of distress. Him admitting his psychosis and that it was all purposeful put everything into a different perspective.

After hanging up, I recall thinking I should tell someone, but who would believe me? It was so insane. The memory of the observer didn't even come back to me until later edits of this book. At the time, I had a feeling of profound terror and the general impression that there wouldn't be any evidence yet, so I would simply come across as the vindictive ex harassing him. I decided then that I had to wait until the right time to tell anyone so I didn't just come across as crazy. I knew he was planning to die at Christmas, so it was best to wait until September. This was a long time to sit on this information.

Unfortunately, my brain couldn't actually deal with full knowledge of this stress, and I had terrible health issues shortly after. In retrospect, I'm guessing they were anxiety-related, but the chest pain was agonizing, and I completely forgot about the cause. I ultimately had surgery on my esophagus to install a self-sealing magnet to help with acid reflux. It eventually turned out I had something more like a too-tight esophagus, but they didn't discover that until the day before surgery and the doctor suggested we proceed anyway. This was probably not advisable as it was fear induced.

I tried various medications to relax my smooth muscles (ones you don't have conscious control of), each of which caused total digestion failure. I did eventually recover but was taking an eighth of a pill that made me sick if I took too much and caused pain if I stopped. That continued for several years after. By the end of that summer, I had almost recovered and resumed my normalish life. Sometimes the only way to keep living is to forget.

I do still wish I had remembered to make that report in September, if for no other reason than to turn things around and ruin one of Blake's plans for once. Perhaps to put a stop to all those assassination attempts as well since there are innocent people who would still be alive if I hadn't failed here as well as millions of dollars of property damage that could have been avoided.

Sometime in November, I started interviewing with a major tech company to be a software engineer. They had a great pay scale and benefits; it's a very well-known and highly reputable organization. I decided to proceed, did some very difficult tests via video conferencing, and was waiting for the results.

Several weeks before Christmas, the recruiter called and informed me that they wanted to proceed with in-person interviews. We scheduled a flight out in early January. Immediately after hanging up the phone, I received a text from Mark, a mutual friend of Blake and mine who had shown me more sympathy than others.

The text read, "Did you hear about Blake's murder?"

Having completely forgotten about the conversation I had with Blake, I was shocked and overwhelmed.

Mark texted because he figured no one would tell me otherwise. After a few exchanges, I decided to call. During the course of our conversation, Mark informed me that he had a sex change operation; it never occurred to me before that he, now she, was potentially transexual. I was placed in a state of shock on two fronts. My friend Mark, now called Kira, was forgiving about being misgendered from time to time during the conversation, but she had to keep correcting me. It was not possible to cognitively process both of these shocks simultaneously.

After hanging up the phone, I briefly felt a sense of relief. It probably lasted for less than a minute. I immediately started doing web research about Blake in a panic afterward. There was almost no information available online. They knew who the killer was because he had dumped Blake's body over a bridge in broad daylight and someone saw him. The river was experiencing drought, so Blake's body didn't go anywhere. The killer had fled and was still being pursued. Some of this information I may have gotten from Mark.

I had a session scheduled with a brand-new mental health provider that evening. I'd been waiting a while for the first appointment. What a remarkable coincidence to have already decided to see someone for help and have the appointment ready.

This shifted the discussion I had planned to have, but he really couldn't cope with this situation. He refused to believe it was all real and wouldn't let me discuss it during our time together.

That's all I needed to talk about at that point. During the course of several sessions, this man steadfastly refused to discuss the murder of my ex-husband. Maybe he didn't believe anything I told him. Apparently, I would get no help from a counselor on this topic.

I slowly collected more information, and I eventually figured out approximately how it had gone down.

24. Final Actions

Blake had given up on pursuing a cure for his disease while living in Atlanta and had no choice but to move back to his hometown. He'd been living there for some time at this point. It was small and boring; it was the last place he really wanted to be. His dreams of becoming a musician had been crushed. He was missing two teeth and was no longer the most attractive man because of it.

He also had HIV so his sex life was risky for others at best. Not that he really cared, but it would look bad to infect another person with the disease, and he absolutely cared about that.

He could easily blame his father, the army, or me as his extremely abusive ex-husband for any number of things; many of them entirely made up or based loosely on the truth. This got him attention and brought him sympathy and sometimes free stuff. Anything not to hold a job. He could continue to perform virtuous works in small, highly public doses that made random strangers think of him as a respectable person.

Those closest to him knew what he was but wouldn't speak of it out of a strange combination of fear, love, and loathing. He knew one thing: dying alone in bed from a slow, degenerative disease was not how he wanted to go out. He wanted to have an interesting death, a warrior's death. So, he came up with a plan.

Blake wanted to be murdered.

He just had to figure out how. Death by cop looked bad. Getting hit by a car wouldn't do. Finally, a breakthrough. He met someone he knew he could manipulate into killing him; a local man who had serious rage issues and had even already killed two people before. Perfect. All he needed to do was ensure he could piss the man off enough to do the job without arousing suspicion and get the timing right.

He learned that his target, John, was living with his father; it was unlikely to be difficult to separate the two, as he was certain someone with two priors had old and very serious issues with his family and loads of emotional instability to exploit. He could figure out the specifics later.

His next phase was to determine the timing. Christmas was perfect. He was always the backup organist at the local church and could most likely ensure he played that year. If necessary, he could offer to do the job for free, but that probably wouldn't be required as the primary organist always wanted off for the holiday anyway. Dying just before Christmas would ensure the entire town was in shock and aware of his death. There wouldn't be time to find a new organist, so they would all have to suffer through the Christmas service fully aware that theirs was missing.

Blake also wanted to know how those closest to him would feel about his death. He told his family he had a rapidly advancing HIV infection and asked what they would think about his passing.

Blake's sister would be relieved, so would his ex-husband. His father didn't really care but would use it to garner sympathy and attention from those around him. His mother would be both terribly hurt and slightly relieved: something they called complex grief. His grandmother, who he had always been good to, was the only one who would truly feel nothing but remorse about his passing. He was slightly sorry about this, but not enough to change anything.

Finally, as late summer approached, it was time to begin manipulating the killer into being close to him. This wasn't very difficult for Blake. He was great at finding out what people liked and giving it to them. John probably did drugs, drank alcohol, and partied. He was also not a popular man because of his criminal record, making him easy to befriend. He was likely in desperation from relative isolation.

Blake simply approached John at a bar and showed him a good time. Not hard at all to pump up someone who was down on their luck, if you know what you're doing. He made sure to suss out anything that would make him happy at this stage. Blake was eventually invited back to John's home for a few hangouts.

There is a saying called "stirring the pot." It means kicking up long simmering tensions between people so they start up old fights that are currently inactive. Blake got to know John and his father so he could figure out what those now ancient fights had been about. Upon learning them, he simply reminded them both about them and ensured they became angry with each other. John's father had been dealing with his son's emotional issues for his entire life and likely went through a lot because of them, so it wasn't very difficult to stir things. The next thing, John was arguing with his father and had been tossed out or simply decided he needed space.

Blake invited John to stay with him as a friend. Although John wasn't gay and had no interest in male parts, it wasn't hard to get him to accept a few blow jobs once they were living together. Just act all submissive and pleasure him a few times. Not long after, John became interested in topping, and Blake was happy to oblige. Blake would be all bottom for John, anything he wanted. Blake infected John with HIV during those first few weeks, but the man had no idea because medical privacy ensured that John was unaware of Blake's condition.

Blake did everything he could to make John happy at this stage. As December rolled around, he procured some meth he could use to get them both high on the night in question. He also ensured there was a gun to keep nearby, one easily available for John to use.

Blake was impatient to be done with it, but bided his time and relished the ruse. Christmas approached, and it was time to execute his ultimate plan. They got high together and were enjoying themselves as the last moments approached. Blake took the gun out.

"What are you doing with that?" John asked.

"Just looking at it. Hey, can I tell you something?" Blake smirked as he waited for an answer. He put the gun down on the table next to John.

"Sure man, you can tell me anything."

"I have AIDS."

"Wait, what?"

"Yeah, I've had HIV for quite a while. I stopped taking my meds some time ago to ensure it would infect you."

"What? Why would you do that? *How dare you—*"

"I wanted to ensure we'd be together forever. This way you can't go anywhere."

If that wasn't enough, Blake could certainly go into interrogator mode. With John's background, that probably wasn't necessary though. Learning that Blake had purposefully infected him with HIV was probably all it took. With the gun sitting right there, John entered a blind rage, picked the gun up and shot Blake in the skull without even thinking about it.

For someone with a history of uncontrolled rage, this was automatic behavior and outside his control. After the deed was done, John realized what had happened and knew the consequences. A third offense meant a lifetime in prison. He had to hide the body and all the evidence.

John called his father in a state of panic. His father, long used to his son's emotional problems, rushed over to help. They came up with an idea: just dump the body in a river together. It would wash away and give them time to escape.

It was morning, and dawn was breaking. No one would be up yet. So, they drove to a local bridge and dumped Blake. They looked down, only to realize the body wasn't going anywhere because the local drought meant there wasn't enough water. They decided to flee together. Little did they know, someone was on the shore and saw the whole thing. In record time, the person reported their suspicious activity to the police. A manhunt ensued.

This met Blake's standard pattern: identify his target, isolate them, manipulate them into being close to him, then make them cognitively impaired and manipulate them into carrying out what action he required. In this case, Blake needed something to piss John off enough to kill him in an act of rage. I am guessing at the specifics, as there simply isn't any information available, and I'm hesitant to bring his family into this to answer questions. I cannot bear to do more research. My life continued anyway, and I unsuccessfully tried to move on.

25. Skeletons in the Closet

I took a trip to Austin over New Year to clear my head and met two women who I hung out with. They invited me to a party at a mansion. One of them told me she wanted me to open up about whatever was happening in my life and then shared something very private about herself. I mentioned that my ex-husband had just been shot. They wanted more information, but I really didn't have any.

We split up for the evening, and they were supposed to text about the party later. I never heard back from them. This repeated itself a few times. I basically found out that you don't talk about the murder in your past because it's too shocking for people. I couldn't speak of it to random people. Even my counselor refused to discuss it! This would mark the last time I mentioned it to anyone for quite a while. I blocked it from my mind in an attempt to move on.

I remember swearing to never let Blake blow my life up again, so I focused on getting the job I had interviewed for prior to learning about his murder. You might describe my focus on code challenges as frantic as I prepared for the only part of the interview that mattered. That proved to be beneficial as they ultimately hired me.

As I was preparing to relocate for the new job, I took a trip to Belize with my father. It's worth mentioning that my father knew about our divorce and about Blake's murder, but at that point even he did not know how bad things had been between Blake and I. No one knew about the attempts on my life except me. It all seemed too crazy to discuss, and I didn't even know where to begin. So, I had been keeping all the true details of our relationship private; I was dealing with it alone. It was largely the farthest thing from my mind though. I would move on from the horrifying events and simply pretend they hadn't occurred.

We enjoyed exploring the jungle together, then visited the crystal maiden, who they learned was male after naming him. We had to swim almost a mile into a cave network and climb along rocks to get there. You were required to leave your shoes behind before entering the cavern they called the Cathedral.

Upon entry, we could understand why it was called this. It was an amazing sight to see. As we entered the small side room where the maiden was, each tourist took an opportunity to briefly look closely at the perfectly crystalized remains.

I gazed up at him; it shocked my spirit again. This pain was far deeper than anything I had experienced. I heard the angry yowl of the torturous suffering his spirit was still in. He wanted to be left alone. This poor soul was a child member of the royal family who had been sacrificed in the most agonizing way possible as a desperate plea to the gods to send rain after a nearly two-hundred-year drought—rain that never came. Mayan civilization collapsed shortly after. I didn't have that sense of torment from the rest of the cavern, though, only when looking directly at the remains.

I feel him communicating as I write these words.

"Don't look at me, don't look at what was done to me. I'm still ashamed, afraid and so angry it fills me with tears. Why Mom and Dad? How could you? Didn't you love me? Wasn't I your special little boy? All for nothing, nothing."

I feel tears well up and pain in my heart for him. He might have taken pride in his sacrifice if only the rain had come.

We finished our trip on a small island. An enjoyable experience all round. Island life seems to be similar everywhere; it's a giant party. Or at least there are enough elements of a party to keep the tourists entertained.

When I went back to Houston, there was some kind of refinery fire they couldn't put out. It filled parts of the city with toxic smoke. There was not much left for me to do but prep for the movers. As I was packing for my cross-country move, I found two last items that belonged to Blake in my possessions. One was his war medals. I had stuffed them away before moving to Houston because I had no idea where Blake was at that point to return them. I sent them to his mother's bakery via USPS because their home address wasn't in the system. Fingers crossed they got there.

There was also a classified document that Blake had left as a poison pill, something that was extremely risky to have and that I could not safely dispose of either. It was about chemical warfare and remained unopened. I took it to the nearest military base.

"Hi, I have this classified document my ex left in my apartment," I said to the man at the front gate as I handed it over to him.

Without even looking at it, he said, "You realize your ex will go to prison for leaving this with you, right?"

"No problem. You can find him underground in a cemetery in upstate New York."

This technically wasn't true, since it was too cold to bury someone in the winter that far north.

Looking slightly shocked, he continued, "Did you read this? If you have opened it, you have legal culpability as well."

"Nope, definitely too smart to do that. There's nothing but nightmares in there anyway, nothing I ever need to know about."

He glanced at the cover and again looked shocked because he could now see a description of the contents.

"Yeah, that's definitely true. You know, they are going to fingerprint this thing. Every page. If anyone has ever read it, they will definitely know."

"Like I said, I never opened it, so I'm not concerned."

"How long have you had it? Are you sure no one else went through it?"

"I had put it into a box of Blake's old things before I left town. When I moved to Houston, I made sure to put it in a cardboard box and then wrapped the box with so much tape it took me almost an hour to open it up. I had forgotten why I did that and was cursing myself as I did; but the wrapping was familiar. When I found the contents, I knew why I'd done that. There was absolutely no way anyone else went into that box or wrapped it up specifically the way I had. No one viewed it, at least since I put it into the box. There was some kid living with us for a while, and there's a chance he went through it, but I suspect not. You're welcome to fingerprint it and I'd be happy to help you track that jerk down and arrest him if he did." I was referring to Talon, who had set me up to be gang raped.

The man let me drive away, and I never heard about it again. I was relieved to be rid of that toxic waste and perhaps just slightly fearful one of my prints was magically on a page somehow due to idle handling. This only lasted a few moments, though, and I put it all behind me as I drove away.

I thought this would end my Blake saga; that I'd be done with him forever. I did not mention the murder to anyone other than my immediate family for several years after and steadfastly blocked anything unpleasant regarding Blake from my mind. Although there was pain, I refused to mourn; this was my shameful past. You don't talk about your murdered ex-husband; it's viscerally disturbing to everyone, and they'll never look at you the same again.

I've since learned that I probably wear much of this experience on my sleeve, but no one recognizes what they're seeing. My spirit is still traumatized and horrified. I distract myself. I think I see evil in places where it doesn't exist and that my mind is still looking for other Blakes out there. While there are certainly some narcissists around, I suspect few were trained to be professional grade by the U.S. government.

Shortly after leaving Houston, two things of no consequence to me happened. Another refinery fire they couldn't put out began, then someone broke into the parking lot of the complex I was living in. That person broke all the car windows. I, meanwhile, took an enjoyable drive west and visited family along the way.

I was so hopeful for a new start. I had no idea that life was about to get even harder.

26. A Poisoned Life

On my way, I met a random young man moving out of the city I was moving into. He talked about being extorted into participating in another list. We discussed the details and both agreed it sounded like a list used to drive people to suicide for fun. It was a mess compared to Houston's list, which had consistent rules that were communicated and enforced. I didn't encounter it for quite a while and eventually forgot about that meeting with the young man. I just blended into the city.

There were people who talked about experiencing systematic harassment and they didn't know why. They talked about being assaulted and their property vandalized, explaining that they were told this had been done to teach them not to mess around with people. All they had done was try to talk to people.

As one man put it, the city was populated by nasty, nasty people. I remember wondering how that could work. How could people who were so mean to others possibly get along with each other?

The following years were chaotic, but I've opted not to tell most of the next part of the story at the moment. Blake's maniacal laughing had been fulfilled by a series of surprising accidents that probably would have killed me if I didn't have an incredible array of survival skills. Many of them are unbelievable and unprovable events because I just bounced along from one thing to another as they occurred in increasingly rapid succession.

I eventually realized that I had developed a severe case of PTSD. One of the symptoms is ignoring horrible things that happen so you can forget them and still experience joy in life. This meant I didn't properly follow up on certain events.

As I write this in 2023, direct attempts on my life by mysterious accidents seem to have abated a while ago. The chaos of survival created problems for me, though. The new city I moved to had someone approach me after about nine months of living there; shortly before the assassination attempts escalated to a feverish pace. This person called himself a kingpin and described something about their list.

This happened about a week after I had survived something extreme and I was slightly worse for wear. I was out of it from what could be described as a hard blow to the head but also stoned and drunk at a club. I lost most of the conversation and all I heard was, "I have a list I use to destroy people's lives for fun. You're required to ignore people on our list for the rest of your life. We also assault and vandalize these people, anything we can do to ruin their lives. We really have fun with it. You're only required to ignore them. You don't have to engage in the assaults."

I was incredibly offended and told him I wanted nothing to do with that. He said I would be assaulted for it and he slandered me on his list with another kingpin friend of his. They both told me that they would enjoy watching my life get ruined but that there was a chance I would one day be removed and ascend to kingpin. If that happened, they would enjoy watching me ruin the lives of the people they had instigated against me. They giggled.

Having deleted most of the memories of my past, so that I could live in the moment and experience happiness, combined with trying to stay alive, I assumed it was part of some insane club trend. I buried my memories of city lists behind a sea of far worse traumas. It also never occurred to me that an entire city full of people would participate in such a thing designed solely to destroy people's lives for fun and would do so over the kind of ridiculous nonsense the man had slandered me with.

There were a series of creepy interactions with these list people. One of the creepier ones was meeting someone I can only describe as a goon. He quite viscerally described enjoying causing pain to others by using this list as an excuse. He knew no greater joy in life than ruining lives through assault and vandalism. I still have an image of this man as a psychopath kept on a chain by the kingpins, to be released upon their victims. These people have taken high school bullying and made it both professional and psychopathic.

After that, people started following me around and telling everyone I was a sexual abuser because I was on the list. This was ridiculous. There were no such allegations about me and such accusations diminished a real problem as well as making light of actual victims.

This happened as I got a viral pneumonia that went long form and made me mentally and physically diminished for about two years; the world itself descended into chaos. The memory problems induced by illness definitely helped with avoiding recalling my past trauma but certainly didn't help navigating the ongoing stuff.

I started taking antidepressants to cover up the malfunctioning of my body and immediately started to grieve Blake. Somehow, I broke a few things of significance to some people by mistake and immediately forgot about the events. I spent the next few months trying to survive my ex-husband's assassins as well as being assaulted by what seemed like random people in the city.

At the time, I assumed it was the kingpins fulfilling their promise. A few people in particular were repeatedly attacking me. One had just assaulted me for the sixth (or so) time, and I had no choice under the circumstances but to hit them back. This particular technique causes no physical injury, but it is viscerally shocking to observe. I walked away from the fight afterward in my typical pacifist fashion.

Everyone who had seen my attacker fly backward assumed I had assaulted him and reported to others that I was a violent criminal. This made the entire city turn against me because I, the victim of their assaults, needed to be driven out to keep them safe. Meanwhile, I have never attacked anyone in my entire life and when met with aggression, work hard not to harm the people trying to injure or kill me. The sole exception was the lynching I mentioned near the beginning of the book, where it was me against over fifty people.

At the time, I kept pushing the list people away because I was focusing on my health and surviving all the assassination attempts. I was truly grieving at this time as well, and the list people felt like nonsense clowns in comparison. After an intense summer that involved me being attacked from all sides over a bunch of stuff that was just made up, the sky turned red due to a slew of forest fires. It was the last straw. I decided to flee the city as we were allowed to work remotely at this point due to coronavirus.

I drove from one end of the country to the other, a 3,000-mile trip, in four days all by myself with a cat. I slept in the car one night, then a hotel and then napped in the car before making the last part of the journey. I remember the smoke only getting thicker until I got through part of Nevada.

Fortunately, time at home with my mother was mentally recuperative and helpful to reestablish a general feeling of safety; the assassins inexplicably chose not to follow me there. Unfortunately, we had to return and the simple act of moving made me sick again (probably due to exposure to dairy).

There were a number of assaults on my work campus when I returned, making me feel like I couldn't participate in socialization at work. I convinced the people to stop, but the trauma remains. They tricked me into trusting people, only to get more information about me so they could use it against me. One found out where I lived so they could break in to destroy the precious artifacts of my world travels. The goon I met shortly after being added to the list then bragged about it while I was at work, hoping I would assault them and get fired. I didn't take the bait.

The extra keys to my apartment and car went missing around this time, and I'm fairly certain they are retaining copies, so I can't feel safe in my own home. I shortly thereafter cleared my name of the supposed assaults, but the initial slander remains, and the kingpins continue to try to destroy my life for fun, making the city I live near entirely unsafe.

One told me they were going to grind me down until I was poor and that they would hunt me no matter where I ran to. They trot out the goon who bragged about vandalizing me to tease me now and then when I am out and about. The worst of the bullies stalk me as well. You would think I could defend myself being a black belt and knowing how, but self-defense only works if you are willing to use it and can always be used against you if you are as skilled as I am.

All of this has been emotionally exhausting and draining. I feel unable to restart a life or trust people locally. The fervent drive I once had for my career has utterly waned. I lack the ambition to find new work of this type. They successfully did as they promised: they finalized the destruction of my already crushed life for fun.

The lawyer I spoke to had heard of this list and strongly recommended I not pursue legal means; I had to find a kingpin to remove me from the list while people assault me for fun simply for being outside. My cat disappeared a while later and I have to wonder if they took him, but I suspect they didn't. It seems like they are trying to create club shooters by targeting people and destroying their lives systematically and making them helpless to do anything else about it.

Several listers I spoke to clearly indicated early on that they knew their list was full of lies but still used it as if it were pure truth. Several admitted that many of the suicides in the city, and even the rest of the country, are directly related to people who were listed and that in many cases the entries were probably just made up, or perhaps as half true as the lies about me were. It would seem that I've been marked by the local mafia, and the kingpins were what the Sopranos called made men.

At various points during all of this, I broke down and told people what I had been through but to no avail. A few seemed amused by my suffering. It seems difficult to climb out of darkness once you're there. It's even harder when you've been systematically isolated for over a decade and have internalized the asocial behavior. People give me strange looks for always being alone.

And I miss Blake from time to time, even though I know he was a toxic man who tried to kill me. At least he made me feel alive when the times were good. I trudge on. Like we all do.

I eventually started supplementing copper and B12 regularly; my memory started to come back shortly thereafter. That process became the inspiration to write this book, which has clarified so much of what happened. My retrospect from what's included here, and what's not, is that the bullies will go on hurting people if I don't do something about it. I have a renewed spirit to ensure they cannot continue causing pain and will try to follow-up on things with more vigor in the future.

My job is going well enough; I have a comfortable and safe position at work even if it doesn't inspire me like it used to. I'm also hopeful that I will make enough money writing this book that I can retire from my tech career and focus on writing more in the future. I have at least two more I could write that would be largely based on truth, as well as some fiction.

Another interesting piece of good news is that during the final edits of this book, I visited Vietnam on vacation. Being in a new place, away from constant victimization that created terror of new connections, has been invigorating and brought out parts of my better self.

One of the side trips I made was to visit the Black Hmong. They are a small tribe in northern Vietnam. While participating in a homestay with a local family, to study their culture and observe their way of life, I was brought to a local shaman. Without being told anything about my past, the shaman told me that the spirit of my spouse was still attached to me and trying to drag me to the underworld. It was creating all sorts of problems for me and holding me back whenever solutions emerged. She said she detached it from me and that as long as I focused on the positives in life, things would improve.

I'm hopeful that I can continue to build something better from the ashes and won't ever stop trying. Time will tell. For now, I'm still partially stuck in the remnants of the spider's web.

27. Final Thoughts

What you love can hurt you more deeply than anything else. This is why you can only ever truly hate what you also love. I both love *and* hate "Blake." I still find myself overcome with feelings of anger, remorse, sadness, and emptiness. I grieve his death while celebrating the removal of him from my life. Writing this book has helped me understand that so much of what he did to me was by design from the very beginning. Hopefully, the understanding it has engendered will eventually help me move on.

Despite the deep pain he caused, I continue to miss him at times and wish that I had done better for him. Any way for him to move on and have a decent life would have been wonderful. He had the potential to become one of the most brilliant organists in recent history if we had found a way to share his incredible compositions with the world.

It might not have mattered. One of the recurring themes in Blake's life was self-sabotage. Whenever things were going well, Blake would suddenly declare that he was unworthy of success due to a little girl he accidentally killed in Iraq. Then our life together would suddenly disintegrate. Yet, this conflicts with his maniacal laughter during our final phone call when he indicated he didn't care if random innocent people died.

I still can't entirely piece him together, even now. He was a deeply conflicted man. Certainly, dying anonymously in bed from a disease is not how he wanted to go. If he couldn't have fame otherwise, he wanted a warrior's death. He absolutely had to leave a mark that people remembered. It being positive was likely less important to him.

As of the time of publishing, I haven't spoken to his family. I understand this book may find its way to you one day, and I am sorry for any pain it causes. I would have liked to pass it by you first, but I was consistently advised against it. Hopefully, my readers will respect your privacy and not track you down and shine a light on you, as I suspect you don't want this attention. You've already been through too much.

Please understand that I wrote this because it was eating me up inside. I had to understand it all somehow. Much of my understanding of what happened occurred while writing it. Blake altered who I am forever. I'll certainly never forget him.

Kirkus Review

A man with the nom de plume Mr. Perpetual Survivor recounts his abusive marriage to a narcissist in this debut memoir.

The author met Blake on a gay dating app: Blake was a 25-year-old Army vet with musical aspirations, and Perpetual Survivor was a 25-year-old computer programmer with a blackbelt in the Korean martial art Tang Soo Do. The two hit it off despite the differences in their personalities—the author was adventurous yet easy-going, more interested in exploring than settling down; Blake, on the other hand, was assertive, with strong opinions and more traditional ideas about relationships. "I got a high-level description of his life that sounded true," recalls PS of their first day together. "He was constantly being victimized by other people and was very good at making you pity him; it was clear he was a lost soul who needed a leg up." Blake's stories of his time in Iraq and Afghanistan, and of his alcoholic father, particularly stoked the author's sympathies. Very quickly, however, Blake revealed himself to be a manipulative schemer. Only a few days after meeting each other, Blake hit PS up for money, threatening to key his car if he didn't give it to him. The author paid him in the hopes that Blake would leave. Instead, Blake moved into his apartment. Attempts to end the relationship and get Blake out of his life proved entirely ineffective. "You committed to me for life," Blake told the confused PS, still only days into their relationship. "You promised to take care of me forever, breaking a vow like that can get you killed." Despite the constant manipulation and financial drain, the author continued to be with Blake, going so far as to move to a new city with him, buy a house with him, and eventually, marry him. By the time PS was to learn whether or not "breaking a vow" really could get him killed, it was almost too late.

There are plenty of stories about toxic relationships with manipulative abusers, but Blake surely sits highly in the ranks of memoir monsters. In addition to Blake's more violent tendencies, he forced PS to buy him a $4,500 pipe organ and even played a role in the author's parents' divorce. His ultimate fate, revealed at the end of the book, is truly wild—if it is to be believed. Perpetual Survivor is not an entirely credible narrator—early in the book, he tells a story about getting injured on a hike and rescued by a female bear who helped drag him back to town (he admits there is "a slight chance it was a fantasy"). He also tells a story about escaping a 100-person lynch mob in Georgia by relying on his skills as a martial artist.

Oddly, these tall tales do not really detract from his narrative, which, after all, is about the experience of being made to feel that you've lost control of your own story. This is a dark work of autobiography, but it is also sensational, insightful, and gruesomely funny.

A madcap survivor's memoir about a monstrous romantic relationship.

Kirkus Reviews

https://www.kirkusreviews.com/book-reviews/mr-perpetual-survivor/surviving-blake/

perpetualsurvivor82@gmail.com

ISBN: 979-8-3485-3878-1